RiPPLE 2021

Kingston University Student Anthology

17th Edition

© Annabel Yates, Benjamin Tickner, Brady Barrow, Caylyn Sheldon, Emily Troy, Farah Nehmé, Fiona Paterson, Grace Watts, Isabelle Gray, Katie Harnden, Kulsy Kashmiri, Laura Broadberry, Matthew Delaney, Molly Hills, Morgan Bratli, Rachel Essex, Rebecca White, Rianna Davidson, Sara Bouda, Shara Cooper, Sim Dyer, Skye Price, Stanimir Dimitrov, Zoë Coleman

The moral rights of the authors have been asserted.

First published in 2021 by Kingston University Press

All rights reserved. No part of this publication may be reproduced or transmitted, in any form or by any means electronic or mechanical, including photocopy, recording, or any information storage and retrieval system, without prior permission of the publisher.

Every effort has been made to fulfil requirements with regard to reproducing copyright material. The publisher will be glad to rectify any omissions at the earliest opportunity.

These stories are works of fiction. Any resemblance to real person living or dead is purely coincidental.

A catalogue of this book is available from the British Library

ISBN 978 1 909362536

Typeset in (typeface)
Photographs / artwork © Kulsy Kashmiri, Zoë Coleman, Farah Nehmé, Brady Barrow, Grace Watts, Rianna Davidson

Editorial and Design by Kingston University MA Publishing Students: Ottavia Caminita, Kulsy Kashmiri, Nasriya Ali Mbarouk, Nikola Trochtová

KINGSTON UNIVERSITY PRESS
Kingston University
Penrhyn Road
Kingston-upon-Thames
KT1 2EE

www.kingstonripple.wordpress.com
Instagram account: @ripple_kingston

CONTRIBUTORS

Managing Editor
Catherine Liney

Assistant Editors
Raven Atkinson
Jack Bartlett

Marketing Team
Maya Conway
Rebecca Hampstead
Laura Kingston
Abbi-Jean Reid

Editorial Team
Laura Broadberry
Clara Ferreyra
Isabelle Gray
Elora Hartway
Zaira Moro
Fiona Paterson
Aleksandra Rybicka

Judging Team
Sarah Bennetts
Shara Cooper
Florence Garnett
Camilla Sansonetti
Laura Strong

Production and Design Team
Ottavia Caminita
Kulsy Kashmiri
Nasriya Mbarouk
Nikola Trochtová

KUP Coordinator
Emma Tait

Cover Design
Kulsy Kashmiri

CONTENTS

Poetry   13

I don't know how to breathe without you by Rachel Essex	14
How I felt this morning by Stanimir Dimitrov	15
Flow by Farah Nehmé	16
A bottle of wine by Isabelle Gray	18
Horror film by Isabelle Gray	19
My artistic colleagues around the world by Stanimir Dimitrov	20
Following the wound by Kulsy Kashmiri	22
How quite is silence? By Emily Troy	24
A Pebble in the Rough by Skye Price	25
Something You Said by Matthew Delaney	26
That's My Pen by Skye Price	27
The Creatives by Skye Price	28
Red flags by Fiona Paterson	29
Snapdragons by Farah Nehmé	30
Obvious by Katie Harnden	31
Hidden Darkness by Anonymous	32
Drops of knowledge by Fiona Paterson	34
Hourglass by Annabel Yates	35

I am a person not a game by Rianna Davidson	36
@JKRowling n' co by Fiona Paterson	37
Circustent by Annabel Yates	40
Drum by Sara Bouda	41
Amalfi by Caylyn Sheldon	42
Modernism by Caylyn Sheldon	43

Prose 45

Below the Crimson Drapes by Morgan Bratli	46
To Have and to Hold by Matthew Delaney	48
Southbank by Grace Watts	56
Breaking the Rules by Sim Dyer	58
The Witching Hour by Shara Cooper	72
Enroe by Brady Barrow	82
The Mogul Attacks by Farah Nehmé	96
A Misremembered Moon by Benjamin Tickner	97
The Wind-Lover by Molly Hills	108
Carrying the Weight of Water By Rebecca White	112
Reflection by Laura Broadberry	120
Untitled by Zoë Coleman	127
Author Bios	128

EDITOR'S NOTE

We are proud to present the 17th annual edition of RiPPLE, showcasing a wide variety of work to celebrate the creativity of Kingston University. The anthology this year includes a range of writing from flash fiction to novel excerpts, poetry and play scripts, as well as the reintroduction of artwork to encompass the very best that Kingston Students have to offer.

Over the past year the world has looked like a very different place to what we are used to, but despite the unique challenges it has brought, it has also highlighted the importance of creativity and coming together. This edition of RiPPLE celebrates every part of life now and before the pandemic, allowing people the freedom to express themselves and see something great come out of a difficult year.

We would like to thank all the people involved, from those who submitted and trusted us with their work to all the people who helped realise our vision of an anthology that encompasses diversity, in both the range of creators and the breadth of material.

This eclectic collection is full of imaginative, experimental and heartfelt work. It has been an honour to experience the creative talent that resides in Kingston and a pleasure to be able to share with you a selection of that talent. I hope you enjoy these pieces as much as we do, I for one can't wait to see where their creative talent takes them.

Yours Sincerely,

Catherine Liney and the RiPPLE Team

FOREWORD

The RiPPLE anthology has become a mainstay at Kingston University, an annual showcase of creativity. In this latest edition we celebrate not only poetry, prose and playwriting but also painting and photography with contributions from students throughout Kingston School of Art.

It has become something of a cliché to reflect that the last year has been a strange one, but there is no doubt that the post-graduate students joining the university last September faced an unprecedented experience. While the act of creation by the contributors has likely been a solitary one, the publication of this anthology is the work of shared endeavour thanks to Catherine Liney, her deputies Raven Atkinson and Jack Barlett, and the large team of volunteers who found a way to create community in a virtual world.

As publishers we have the privilege of helping others bring their work to a wider audience and I am proud that we are now able to amplify the voices of our talented students beyond the university, to a global audience, thanks to the opportunities afforded by print-on-demand technology. Indeed you may well be reading this copy having ordered it from an online retailer thousands of miles away from Kingston.

The slimness of the volume belies its content and the range of voices within: from the quiet introspection of 'How I felt this morning' to the violence of 'Drum'. For some of our writers it's been a lifelong habit, while for others the recent lockdown has been the inspiration to create.

To misquote Kulsy Kashmiri's poem, while words may be nothing but ripples, together they can form a wave.

Emma Tait

Publisher, Kingston University Press

March 2021

Rachel Essex
I don't know how to breathe without you

'Are you okay?'

I'm drowning
in waves of a familiar face.
It used to smile at me every morning
and kiss me every night.
He is the tide,
here one moment and gone the next.
He crashes around me on the shore,
taking me in once before gripping my waist
and pulling me out to sea.

He buries me beneath his surface,
the waves lapping over me,
again, and again.
I want to fight against his currents,
because if I don't, I'll die.
If I do, I'll be free from his hold
and it will all be over.
But I'm not sure which is worse.

I struggle against his riptide,
as he fills my lungs with water.
My final seconds are of his face,
the memories of what once was
and what would never be.

Stanimir Dimitrov
How I felt this morning

'Hey, how are you?'
'I don't really know...'
'Why, what's going on?'
'I don't really know...'
'Ok, express it how you know.'
'Well…

...my coffee tastes like morning
which is good yet I don't want food
I'm making sausage rolls
which I hate but it's the only thing on the shelf
and when Mum asked
I needed to say I ate

I am sitting on the couch
staring at a blank screen
all my games inside
ready to make me angry
and want to scream
but even that I don't want

What I want is nothing

I have the room to myself
and I should be happy
but I feel so lonely and
I want someone to hold me

My coffee tastes like morning
yet my mouth is dry as hell
but when they ask if I'm okay
I can't even tell.'

Farah Nehmé
Flow

Isabelle Gray

A Bottle of Wine

One Glass:
The devil weighs down my shoulder,
Whispering temptations.
But my head is light and his
Words are dust.

Two Glasses:
The ghosts become solid.
A weight on my chest.
Dragging my heart through my stomach,
Into my legs,
Turning them to jelly beneath me.

Three Glasses:
I can barely stand as I face myself in the mirror.
Bloodshot eyes meet bloodshot eyes,
The person looking back...
Unrecognisable to me: a skeleton.

Four Glasses:
I am kneeling on the floor
A puddle of bro ken glass and cracked skin
The world is crimson and s p l i n t e r e d glass
The taste of iron on my lips.

The Bottle:
I dream that the wine is my Styx,
If I drink enough,
If it consumes every part of me -
I won't feel it anymore.
And yet, I am Priam at Zeus' Altar,
And it feels like a mercy.

Isabelle Gray

Horror Film

He asked me to watch a horror film with him,
Offered to hold me close and cover my eyes
When the ghosts jumped out and scared me.
I told him, I don't need to watch *The Conjuring*
To see ghosts dancing at the end of my bed and
In the corners of my mind.
I live my life in black and white,
In shadows and ghosts.
I don't want to watch a horror film,
When your love is tinted purple;
The light in your eyes and the rainbow in your smile
When you hold me in teal;
The whispering of dreams in the moonlight,
and the words you never tell another soul.
I told him, I don't need you to show me a horror film,
When you are the only escape from mine.

Stanimir Dimitrov
my artistic colleagues around the world

Good Morning to

the ones sipping coffee
every minute to stay awake
bringing tobacco to flame
to fill in their heavy pasts
the same ones pouring hearts out
on a blank piece of paper

the ones stretching out to
move the shadows and
talk beauty with their bodies
bouncing beats through their veins

the same kind of people
whose ears soak in music
and their vocals fill other hearts
making people shiver

all the pliant hands
shaping a nothing out of clay
into a something
beautiful in its own way

people whose eyes
capture every view that is scenic
and hold the brushes tight
painting the world anew

every single outcast
spraying walls for the fun of it
but also to create something
that is for society an artistic gun

all the digital children
shifting keys and mice hard
just to create a different
virtual kind of art

everyone else I just so happen to forget
but no one else should
for we don't want them to regret
that they're born for an industry
where people have to fight
to show the world that they have
what others call an artistic delight
a world where money helps none
nothing covers the expense
of hours spent in darkness
thinking what do to and change next
but people will see your art
and praise you for your ways
of taking something beautiful
and leaving it behind with your name

now even if you're alone
after a day filled with failed attempts
to create this beautiful art that's
begging to escape your brain
and no one excites over your work
lay down and rest
for tomorrow is another chance to
breathe and use your gift

Good Night

Kulsy Kashmiri
Following the wound

I float endlessly.
Like a fish in the sea, ambling existentially.
I cannot feel my lungs anymore,
As my breath is in front of me.
I try to reach out, but it passes through me.
I'm still musing in the water,
Back balanced against fresh waves that vibrate.
The sea is talking to me.
His whispers tickle my flesh and kiss my scars.
Open wounds and memories swirl around me, gathered and waiting.
I realise that these words are nothing but ripples,
and I can't help but smile.
Because I hate the water,
I always feared I would drown.

Emily Troy
How quiet is silence?

How quiet is silence?
I'd quite like to know.
After everyone's ceased talking,
Is there much further to go?
Do you have to stay still?
Cover your eyes and ears,
Is solitude required?
After the talking stops,
When your thoughts all settle and the anticipation drops.
Will I have to confront my fears?
When you're all alone,
Looking at the ceiling, trying to avoid your phone.
How quiet is silence?
Do you really want to know?
It's quietly crushing and in no rush to go.

You put a chapter in my book
That I did not approve
You decided on the hook
Bent the tale towards you.

Stain marks on my pages
That were swirling in your ink
Blotted sacrifices
Blocking my ability to think.

Momentarily I sat back
My words scripted for me
Unaware of who I was
Lost in my own story.
The characters don't make sense here
This is not the plot I had in mind
A chapter can never be undone
But it can be left behind.

You were a part of my story
I've crafted pages since then
You are no longer the antagonist
You no longer have the pen.

I am writing my own tale now
And the hero may be flawed
But she's so full of freedom
Overcome what she's endured.

Sometimes I hesitate
On who I should write in
I'm scared that someone might
Try to take my pen again.

But now I know how to
Regain the narrative's control
I will never be a second thought
In a story that's my own.

Skye Price
That's My Pen

Matthew Delaney
Something You Said

(This one's for you)

Heartfelt dreams,
Conspired through synthwave keys.
Memories in melodies,
All in the echoes of the words
That your soul confessed.

Each riff, a testament to time,
Obscurity's a crime.
Unheard till resurrection.
But brother dearest,
Don't go thinking it's all over,
I still hear you.
It was something that you said.

Pull me in.
Your voice is left behind.
Frozen back in time.
Your treasure beyond gold.
Your stories to be told.
Though now silent, you inspire.
It was something that you said.

Heartfelt dreams,
Conspired through synthwave keys.
Memories in melodies,
All in the echoes of the words
That your soul confessed.

A legacy of notes and dreams.
Your voice will sing again.

Heartfelt dreams,
Conspired through synthwave keys.
Memories in melodies,
All in the echoes of the words
That your soul confessed.

That your soul confessed.

Skye Price
A Pebble in the Rough

The smooth pebbles you see
lay on picturesque shores and
translucent riverbeds,
began as rough stones. They
journeyed through turbulent
waters, bashed and bruised. The
world around them chipped at
their surface, altering them
forever, arriving far from where
their journey began, and yet
we admire them all the more.
Shining.
Basking in their new design.

Skye Price
The Creatives

Dreamer, believer, Instagram feeder, story
teller, weaver, never felt freer, spinning
your wheel, you're a seeker, teacher, presented
with a problem, you become a thinker, a give
me a moment and I'll have an answer, situation
solver, never give in, achiever.

A note in a phone, voice memo, writer,
drawer, composer, a tryer,
to aim even higher, hand sew your wings
and fly even further, you're an inspiration
finder, a stark reminder

that we are more than our day jobs
and more than our binders.

A handful,
A mindful,
A mouthful of fire;
You are a creator,
A soarer,
A flyer.

Here we are again,
caught in the habitual trance of the club,
using our hearts as compasses.

Stairs littered with red flags meet colour-blind fingers that see evanescent greens.
Pulled in by magnetic lust, we taste the inside of each other's throats and pretend to find rich flavours.

We inject chilli-tingling spices into blandness and smooth over the edges with silky cream.
We dance in imaginary texture and almost find sustenance in each other's emotional vomit,
Gaping our mouths like baby birds.

Fiona Paterson
Red flags

Snapdragons

Katie Harnden
Obvious

It's pretty obvious that something hidden is happening. There is an atmosphere of a cover up, a fresh looking fruit, rotten inside.

Reaching skyscrapers, with no inhabitants, shops without soul or creativity.

Replica after replica, mirroring a realty which isn't their own. A false sense of success shapes each and every face. White pale skin from deadened escape.

Masking false hope in individual, designer items. Dressed to perfection, crumbling from rejection.

A stage, a toy town, masked with bridges and an endless skyline. Expectancy around every corner, bleeding, false satisfaction and pride.

Nannies replacing mummies, cameras replacing certainty. Criminality disguised, unknown, cranes constructing future.

Distinguished class division in every glimpse, reminding one of their place and position.

Children, blissfully unaware of surrounding falsity. Security, guarding unknown streets.

High walls, clean pavements, trimmed hedges, closed eyes.

Paid satisfaction with heartbeat of pleasure. Stripped sense of value, hollowed, gaping pride. Lust, driven vendors on every stand.

A hidden scream for understanding with every shake of a hand.

Anonymous
Hidden Darkness

The darkness within penetrates like a knife. This house will know no peace.
Where does it begin, where does it end, when love learned is pain?
In a half-parented home, something internally brews,
This becomes the norm. There's nothing like knowing your breed-
The evil men do, some mothers too, cloaks one in despair.
Where do we go, as nights grow cold, the mind begins to crumble?

Reflecting as hairs grow grey, life's stages can cause you to crumble.
You may never get passed that troubled past, that really took the piece;
or chunk, or almost all of you, what's left is shattered despair.
You want to escape, but where to go, you stare through the windowpane
It comes, it goes - imposter syndrome, the first few were the wrong breed:
They're full bloods, then came half ones, royally not knowing what brews.

It grows with you, it goes with you: home-grown blended brews.
Like Usain Bolt - some trained to win, others like buildings crumble.
Intertwined crushed grapes from vine, eventually all shall breed.
Is there an escape, when you leave that place, your haven that isn't peace?
It's a trap door, being locked in your thoughts, everyone has dirty panes.While the clock ticks, calendars shift, there's limitations to despair

At times you look down, sometimes you're up, your reality is despair.
Nonetheless, are you more or less carrying this timely bruise
Silently - alone, reminiscing on the pain,
Tossing and turning, as your world begins to crumble.
You grow your own, watered and honed, this house shall know peace.
Loud as a chorus, heaped praise at the doorstep, they're all the perfect breed.

This isn't the end, is there a mend to the irrelevance of a breed?
The rivalry between siblings transcends age, reminding you of despair
Each and every year. Is there a family construct that's peace?
When you're trained so well and all can tell those bruised
Apples fell from the wrong seed. Unions tear, relationships crumble
And cancer eats from the core. Healing's essential escapism from the pain

    There are always ways, you self-medicate: that sedates the pain.
None of this matter's, what really matters is knowing, you're a bad breed!
        Like Botox, trying to freeze faces that crumble
           stop baring your soul in despair.
When every response, adds a new bruise,
        Are you addicted to losing your peace?

Eventually time's up, the world won't stop, don't be beaten by despair
And know yourself, above all else, before contempt boils like brews.
Balloons they pop - releasing hate, only forgiveness brings joy and peace.

Fiona Paterson
Drops of knowledge

Ability conscious insecurity complex.
Am I learning the right things?
Extracting drops of knowledge from an earth-sized coconut, full to the brim.
And I know it's not enough to just feel thirsty but the more I drink, the more dehydrated I become.
Every thrum of milk perspires from the shell onto my tongue; leaking with composure.
The fathomless white spume gurgles on above me, dripping only elements.

It's clear that I would drown under the weight of it all, that I'd vomit lakes of thought, rivers of rap and seas of history.
But is it enough to hack at the sides and taste new perspectives when I cannot ingest them all?

The ocean makes me feel so god damn small.

Annabel Yates
Hourglass

When
the world died
all knew it was coming
tears spilled from bare souls
strangers clutched strangers
the silence had begun
all screaming
stopped.

All
screaming stopped
the silence had begun
strangers clutched strangers
tears spilled from bare souls
all knew it was coming
when the world
died.

Rianna Davidson
I am a person not a game

Fiona Paterson
@JKRowling n' co

God my tits meant so much to me when I was young,
The obsession, like - where will they spring from? And when?
I got a bra because I'm of that age, that stage when it's weird to
feel cloth against chest without more cloth against 'breast'.
But here's the thing, here's what I enjoyed about puberty: I felt
connected to my body, to my mind, it meant unity.
I was told it was natural.
And given advice,
Saw myself in my peers and felt legitimised.

My questions would be answered without doctors being called.
My gender was accepted without government reform.
When the blood in my pants tied a knot in my womb,
My hormones were rebalanced with a pill to consume.

Ya wombs in knots - take the pill.
Ya boyfriend's hot - take the pill.
Ya face got spots - take the pill.
Side effects? Meh it's chill.

We can't block your hormones yet, you're too young to understand,
We can't fiddle with your hormones just because you're sad.
Doctor to patient: the side effects are blah.
The side effects, the side effects, the side effects are…
We can't be impatient, we're six months down the line,
We have to know for certain, we're waiting for a sign.

A sign that reads:
I AM QUEER I AM QUEER
PUBERTY IS MY BIGGEST FEAR.

…

transphobia is weird bro, like
imagine being annoyed at existence
imagine thinking a trans woman is out to trick you
LOL
She's just living her life
actively avoiding c**ts like you
but all womanhood comes down to is the vagina, right?

ha   ha   ha

Imagine thinking that cis women deserve a 'safe space' away from trans women… and imagine justifying this as feminism, Jesus Christ…

Who are you trying to escape? Because I'm pretty sure
the woman-beating men are pickling in the toxic sauce of
masculinity,
So probs wouldn't pop a dress on to distress when there are
streets and clubs and bars and gyms and cars and home after
literal home for them to plunder.
And I wonder, does your womanhood look different to their
womanhood when seen through hateful eyes?
Or do they just see prey?

And I wonder what you mean when you say 'safe space' and
who you think you are protecting.
Your selective protection wreaks of rejection and you justify this
violence with fear???
You justify this violence with *FEAR?!*
Oh, sweet Bigotry, how well you hide beneath Fear's cloak.
And I wonder how you feel beneath your politics. Warm? Safe?
Solid?
Comfy in the knowledge that people will speak out for you?
Whilst you waste your breath speaking out against women who
are different, and a bit the same.
Women whose abuse is different, and a bit the same.
Women whose needs are different, and a bit the same
Women who are not warm, nor safe, nor solid, but speak out for
you time and time again.

Nobody loves her;
She has feet,
gills
and fins.

Girl, dressed in pink;
swimming against too-thick glass,
wide-eyed little fish.

In her glass box
full of water;
bubbles floating free.

Crowds swallowed under red and yellow;
dripping candy on the outside,
blank eyes blink on empty faces.

Cackling children pummel glass
but yank coins back again,
angry adults call her fake.

Nobody remembers her;
too tired to swim,
bubbles pop around her
floating upwards, belly first.

Annabel Yates
Circustent

Sara Bouda
Drum

Crack said the drum,
As the light rose,
Against the toes,
That marked a line across the dirt.

Crack said the drum.
The crash of silver,
Like falling water,
As the heel stamped out its anger.

Crack said the drum.
Those parting thighs,
Those writhing sides,
As hips moved and twisted faster.

Crack said the drum,
Flames leapt higher,
Hands spoke louder,
The silent darkness drawn in closer.

Crack said the gun.
The fear of death,
The spread of red,
The scream of pain burned deeper.

In the dirt beneath our feet,
The scattered dead,
The shattered thread,
A broken line across the earth.

Caylyn Sheldon
    Amalfi

Pierces and pricks the saltwater sea
Off the coloured coast of Amalfi,
Where tourists flow like busy bees.
But tonight, the breeze sings quietly
As I inch further and further in.

Pinches and pries from blackened skies
Disguising water and whatever innit lies.
Past my open lips and embracing my eyes,
it flows and fills me down to surmise
How the water cold feels better than sin.

Pulls and pushes the current, leads
my willing self to a world I cannot see,
where unknowns thrive and breathe
in ways I haven't and never shall be,
so long as wind whirls and time spins

Perfect and pacific in the disguise
of Mediterranean shores, though I'd advise
You'd swim back before you realise
That you have not the strength to rise
From the selfish sea's grasp within.

Caylyn Sheldon
Modernism

If I'm to be remembered,
I have to come up with
the next best thing.

I slam my face into the
keyboard and win the
Pulitzer Prize.

A band-aid's on my chin
because I wrote something
that hurt too much.

An ardent fan gets tattoos
of my bruises on his face.
So dedicated.

In poetry classes, they'll try
hitting their heads on keys
to imitate me.

There'll be anthologies of all
my genius and a portrait of
my broken nose.

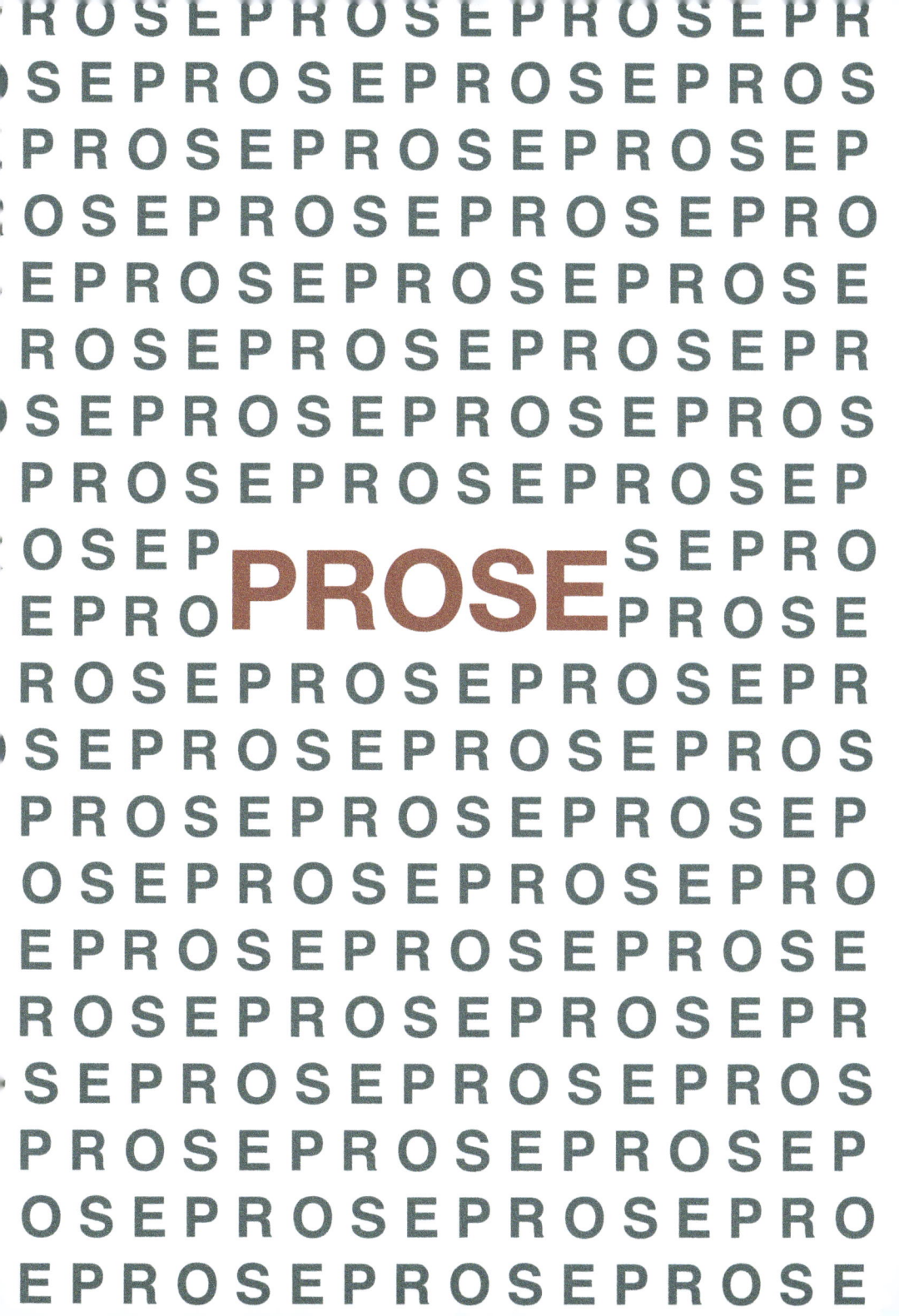

Morgan Bratli
Below the Crimson Drapes

My fingertips prickled with might. Me, strong and unbeaten by that - a puny, disgusting and motherless beast. The curtains draping the window would cover its wounds - why it even bore the same colour as the pouring rivers from the creature's neck!

I needed fresh clothes. Fresh clothes and a comb to straighten my hair. Where to even find such things? The manor seemed twice in size when I sealed away the hideous monstrosity behind me. A vast labyrinth of halls, twisting stairs and settled dust, but the smell was always sweet, like a jar of fermented apple or perfectly ripe grapes. It made my head swirl and my thoughts mush and it took me half an hour to find a cupboard holding my own clothes. But I found them. Oh, how the dry garments clasped my flesh to perfection, from every seam to every line, not a single crease to be found! The thought of being hugged by untainted fabric after having felled the beast sent me into an unrivalled euphoria. The world rested so pleasantly in the pit of my unyielding palm.

I was struck by an absorbing thought accompanied by most vivid images, which left me wondering for some time. How long would the beast lie bleeding? Until it resembled a dried plum? A rotting crow, a festering fly? Perhaps it would bloat and burst apart as a beached whale? Fascinating questions and an excellent idea to do some reading on the subject.

The clanging bell struck to mark the hour's passing and with it came the timely creaking of the front door.

'My love?' I yelled.
'Yes, darling! It is only I,' the walls said, carrying his voice past hall and stair.
'Come, my love. I am up here!'
But he came not for me. He went straight for the door hiding the beastling.
'Why is this locked, my dear?'
'Oh, the thing must be asleep, surely.'
'Open it, will you?'
'Never mind the thing. Tonight is ours. Is that truly so terrible?'
Before my words reached his eardrums, the door was on the floor in a cloud of soot. I stood behind him, putting my arms around his waist and locking my fingers. Inside me, right to very depths of my belly was a fire growing violent. 'It sleeps. Only us, now.'

His face was stricken pale as chalk and I heard his tongue flapping around in his mouth as he searched for words to convey the magnitude of his love for me. The kind of love that could travel beyond all the dimensions of the cosmos.

But he could not force the words beyond those sugary lips I ached to taste again. He breathed as a steam engine - no, as an afeared pig deprived of air! The thing on the floor shifted. I saw the crimson drape swell and settle by the beast's mouth.

And then I understood with a sword of ice impaling the end of my spine, the breathing came not from the lungs of my love, but from the creature hidden below the drapes I wished never had crawled from my loins!

Matthew Delaney
To Have and to Hold

'Are you still mad at me?'

Richard sat in the passenger seat, motionless, facing the rolling horizon. The tension in the car was suffocating, barely tempered by Julia's attempts to indulge in late night radio, fiddling with the tuner dial as she steered through the silent night.

'I didn't mean it. *Honest*. You know I didn't. You know I love you, right?'

Tears welled in Julia's eyes, blotting her near-perfect mascara, while her husband continued to offer no visible sign of surrender. It had been silent between them for a while now; *she* had been angry and now *he* wouldn't answer. Like many a love, theirs was no stranger to storms; though how bitter the breeze.

Julia caressed Richard's shoulder before refocusing on the road, the evening breeze spiriting hints of her husband's musky aftershave through the car as it crawled through the window.

'Richard, *please*. I'm sorry,'

Again, Richard refused to answer. Julia knew all-too-well of Richard's stubbornness, along with other fiery aspects of his character; yet still she loved him, somehow they worked, fitting together like two desperate pieces in life's messed-up jigsaw.

Theirs had been a simple wedding; with little put-by and with Richard's penchant for cards, it had been far from the princess wedding that Julia had dreamed of as a child. Second-hand sentiments and upstaged in-laws seemed to tarnish the charm of the otherwise whimsical old church affair. But even so, it had been honest and filled with the genuine affection the two shared for each other. They were flawed but they were human and they were in love.

Richard wasn't usually the silent type but tonight circumstance had dealt him a different hand. Though only inches away, Julia felt Richard was more distant than ever.

Pulling into a petrol station, Julia parked the car in a side bay and switched off the engine. She ran her fingers over the steering wheel, gathering her thoughts with a cleansing breath before checking her hair in the rear-view mirror.

'I need a drink. Do you want anything?'

Richard remained silent, his eyes reflecting his reluctance to be there at all.

'Suit yourself.'

Exiting the car, Julia walked across the forecourt, relieved at the temporary release. The strain was telling on her brow, each crease confessing the details her mind sought to avoid. Inside the forecourt shop, the blustery air conditioning and eerily upbeat instrumental music offered a slither of comfort. Here, she was anonymous in such transient refuge; free within the concrete cage.

Melting into the aisles and their fluorescent glow, Julia enjoyed every second away from the car.

A glance at the chiller cabinet drew Julia's attention to Richard's favourite brand, the one with the retro rocket-ship on the front; lemonade with hints of summer berries. Julia stroked a finger down the nearest bottle as a stray tear ran down her right cheek.

Gingerly approaching the tills, Julia placed her small selection of items down by the cashier. The cashier was middle-aged with volumized hair fresh from the 1980s and a face that implied she had regretted it every day since. Their eyes met for a moment, each sharing defensive smiles. Julia looked past the cashier towards the car, her expression betraying the nonchalance posed so expertly by that well-rehearsed face. 'If only', 'why', 'what if', 'maybe'; the questions flashed through Julia's mind. How had one mistake led to this? Why did this time have to be so different? It simply wasn't fair.

Rain tapped against the long exterior window as Julia stared outside; a little at first, followed by heavier streams. She could just about see Richard sitting within the shadows. He didn't wave or acknowledge her. Julia wished he would.

'Long night?' remarked the cashier.

'Something like that,' Julia offered defensively, keeping a forlorn vigil out the window.

Indulging in conversation whilst the rain mesmerised and soothed her broken mind, mirroring the tears Julia wouldn't allow herself to cry.

'Who is *he*?' asked the cashier, following Julia's gaze outside.

Julia took a deep breath, composing herself as the cracks felt large enough to devour her whole. She had to get through this, *somehow.* Putting on her bravest face, Julia held up her hand to show the sparkling ring, fiddling with it awkwardly once lowered. The cashier nodded.

'*Ah.* Yeah, I had one of those once. Pain, aren't they?' the cashier offered, her tone experienced and raspy.
Julia sighed under her breath, offering only a shallow and sympathetic smile.

'Ya' know, I had a rule with mine; if it was something I couldn't change then it was something I wouldn't worry about.'

Suddenly the forecourt lights flickered, breaking Julia's

concentration on the car.
'But what if -'

Julia's voice trailed off, her throat seizing up. The cashier was gone, the lights now flickering haphazardly; the dishevelled shop surrounding her worlds apart from the one it had been seconds before. Peering across the counter, the graffiti now scrawled across the cabinet doors offered chilling credence to the fear paralysing Julia's heart - *'he'll tell them'*.

Scared, Julia ran back to the car, fumbling for the right key before diving inside and locking the door again behind her. Through the wisps of moonlight and flickering fluorescent hue, she caught the glint in her husband's watchful eye, his gaze reflecting a silent judgement she knew was burning away inside him. Deep down part of her felt she deserved it but this was a battle of wills.

Starting the car, Julia abruptly drove off the forecourt and onto the lonely road that awaited her, so still and absent of life under the moonlight. An initial glance in the rear-view mirror failed to show the petrol station at all, confusing Julia while merely adding to the troubles she was travelling with. Even a quick glimpse over the backseat confirmed the same; the station was gone from the horizon, as if never there at all. All Julia could do was keep driving further into the night, clinging to the hope that eventually the darkness would relent.

At first, she tried using the radio as a distraction but every song that came on either evoked a bittersweet memory or seemed like a sarcastic jibe from some higher power; even the radio hosts offered nothing but cuttingly ironic commentary that Julia couldn't help but relate to.

A frustrated twist of the dial preceded another late-night station to fill the car.

Another twist flooded the car with the tell-tale riffs of '*Every Breath You Take*', leading Julia to side-eye across at her husband.

A few times Richard's phone buzzed, only to be ignored completely by its owner; not even a cursory glance. Julia hated this change in him. It was a far cry from the sociable rogue she'd fallen in love with. Finally, Julia turned off the radio and decided to face the problem she couldn't escape from.

'I really wanted this to work, Richard. I wish… I wish you'd forgive me,'

Richard refused to relent, upholding his silence while Julia sobbed; the tears obscuring her view through the windscreen momentarily until she dug deep and regained fragments of her composure.

'I really am sorry. You know if I could take it back I would,' she offered lowly.

Julia kept talking the rest of the journey, confessing her every love and regret as her husband sat patiently beside her, silently absorbing each detail.

Eventually the lonely road, widened to include vestiges of civilisation - signs, buildings, other people; yet somehow Julia felt sadder than ever. She knew what reaching the hotel meant. Pulling into the driveway, she sighed. After securing the handbrake, she reached out for Richard's nearest hand and squeezed it tenderly, the lonesome sorrow echoed across her otherwise youthful face.

'Well I guess this is it then,' said Julia, staring hopelessly at Richard's equally forlorn expression, 'Goodbye Richard.'

She rustled his hair one last time, allowing herself one final moment, even if uninvited. Her fingers now stained, Julia casually wiped her hands on a tissue from the glove compartment, discarding the crimson truth in the tray beneath the central console. Wiping her eyes, she stepped outside the car, wore her bravest smile and handed the car keys over to the young valet. Julia must've been halfway up the grand entrance stairway when the valet's screams filled the air.

'He's dead! *Help*! He's dead!'

Those few seconds were enough to send the frightened valet fleeing from the car, a huddle of people beginning to curiously gather around him. Turning her head to face the inevitable truth, Julia sighed once more.

'Yes, I know.'

Grace Watts
Southbank

Sim Dyer
Breaking the Rules

BREAKING THE RULES - Sim Dyer

CAST LIST

Bartender: Woman, in her late 20s
Paul: Man, in his late 30s
Shannon: Woman, in her early 30s
Compliance Officer: Man, in his mid 40s

   VOICES
Protestors off stage

ACT 1
Dim lights open the stage. There is a bar with two stools in front of it, as well as two round tables, each with two chairs. Behind the bar, a bartender sits tapping away on her phone. Bob Marley's Three Little Birds plays lightly in the background.
Paul walks onto the stage in a blue three-piece suit and goes over to the bar. He pulls out the stool while removing his mask

and sits down, dumping the mask on the counter.

Paul: Double JD on the rocks.

The bartender, without looking up from her phone, points to a bottle of hand sanitiser on the counter.

Paul: But I just washed my han-

The bartender looks up and stares into Paul's eyes before pointing to the bottle of sanitiser for the second time. Paul sighs and pumps some of the sanitiser into his hands. Slowly he rubs his hands together while glaring at the bartender, whose back is now to him, as she prepares the whiskey.
The bartender turns around and puts the whiskey in front of Paul while giving his mask a look of disgust. As he picks up the drink, she whips a pen from her back pocket and uses it to lift the mask by its strings.

Paul: (slamming his glass back down) What the hell are you-

Bartender: It's a disposable (she drops the mask in the bin).
Paul: And I would have disposed of it when I got home.

Bartender: Rules are rules.

Paul: Whose rules?

Bartender: Don't you watch the news?

Paul: But yesterday-

Bartender: Yesterday was yesterday. Today is today. We are evolving.

Paul sits back down, shaking his head and downs the whiskey before pushing the glass back towards the bartender.

Paul: (warily) Make it a double-double.

Enter stage, Shannon dressed in a grey business suit and carrying a laptop bag. She walks over to the bar and sanitises her hands. The bartender, who has just given Paul his whiskey, smiles.

Bartender: Hey (she turns to the shelf behind her and reaches for a bottle). Merlot?

Shannon: Yes please.

The bartender places the bottle on the bar and reaches above herself for a glass.

Bartender: Two glasses or one?

Shannon: Just the one (yawns). It's been hectic.

Bartender: (sympathetically) I can only imagine.

The bartender begins to open the bottle, but Shannon waves her hand.

Shannon: I'll pour it when I'm settled.

Bartender: No problem.

Shannon takes the glass and the bottle and walks over and sits at one of the tables. She takes her laptop out and places it on the table, then switches it on.
Paul has been watching this exchange with a slight look of confusion on his face. The bartender notices.

Bartender: What?

Paul: Do you just hate men?

Bartender looks taken aback.

Paul: I got hostility and she got (feminine voice) how was your day.

Bartender: (assertively) You (pause) were breaking the rules.

Paul: But she wasn't even wearing a damn mask.

Bartender: She's exempt.

Paul: Why?

Bartender: It would be rude to ask.

Paul: So how do you know?

Bartender: Well, she came in without a mask.

Paul: Oh, I see (nods his head). So you're assuming she's exempt?

Bartender: She knows the importance of following rules.

Paul: How so?

Bartender: She's a reporter.

Paul shakes his head and holds out his hand.

Paul: Can I get the bill?

Stage light goes down.

Act 2

Dim lights open the stage.

The bartender is alone cleaning down the bar. Ghost Town by The Specials is playing in the background.
Enter Paul in a black suit and no mask. He walks over to the bar and makes a point of sanitising his hands before sitting down. The bartender stops cleaning and looks at him.

Paul: Double whiskey please.

Bartender: No mask?

Paul: I thought it was rude to ask.

Bartender: But yesterday-

Paul: Yesterday was yesterday, today is today. I (pause) am evolving.

Bartender: But-

Paul: (loudly) drink please.

Bartender: I'm not a clairvoyant (pause). Which drink?

Paul: (irritated) The same drink I had yesterday and the day before!

Bartender: Relax... I had to check since today you're... evolving.

The bartender pours the drink and places it in front of Paul. She looks him up and down.

Bartender: Coming from a funeral?

Paul: This is a funeral.

Bartender: What you on about?

Paul: It's a global funeral.

Bartender: Well, you're here and I'm here, so stop exaggerating.

Paul: (sighs) Again – making assumptions.

Bartender raises her eyebrows.

Paul: Where is here?

Bartender: Here (pause) in a bar (pause) in London.

Paul: And where is London?

Bartender: In the U.K.

Paul: And where is the U.K.?

Bartender: Erm... on the planet Earth?(she laughs nervously)

Paul: But how do you know we're on the planet Earth?

Bartender: Well science-

Paul: Awww science (he holds up his hand). So, some scientists told you we are on the planet Earth, so of course it must be true, right?

Bartender: (defiantly) Right - what are you getting-

Enter Shannon onto the stage pushing a coffin on wheels and with a camera holder slung over her shoulders. She pushes the coffin up to the bar and smiles at the bartender.

Shannon: (breathing heavily) Hi.

The bartender says nothing and instead stares at the coffin with her mouth wide open.

Shannon: Don't worry it's empty (looking at the coffin). I got a good deal. You know (pause) just in case...

Paul: That's absurd.

Shannon: Nobody was talking to you (she flicks her hair back). But glad to see you dressed for the occasion.

Paul: (under his breath) Morbid.

Shannon: Makes it easier. If I (she points to herself) or any of you (she points at Paul and then the bartender) drops. Then we're prepared.

Bartender: Except there has to be a post-mortem.

Shannon: Says who? Everyone knows we are all going to succumb. It's just a matter of time. And nobody's doing post-mortems. Do none of you watch the news? (pause) Then you should know that these (gestures to the coffin) are getting harder and harder to come by.

Paul:(peers at the coffin) Bit small.

Shannon: It's fine.

Paul: I wouldn't fit.

Shannon pulls the lid off and props it up against the bar.

Shannon: Let's see then.

Paul: (scoffs) I'm not getting in that thing.

Bartender: Go on (she turns and grabs the whiskey bottle). The next ones on the house - unless you're scared (she sniggers)

Shannon: Let me help.

She walks behind Paul and reaches towards his suit jacket. He shrugs her off.

Paul:(loudly) 2 metre distance love. I thought you knew the rules.

Shannon: (rolls her eyes) We're breathing the same air.

Paul stands up and takes off his jacket, laying it neatly on the stool. He inspects the coffin and then goes to the head and crouches down to lift it. He looks up at Shannon expectedly. She hurries to the foot of the coffin and together they lift it onto the ground. Both stand and look at the coffin in silence. The bartender clears her throat loudly. Paul looks at her.

Paul: Make sure it's a double-double.

Paul climbs into the coffin slowly.

Shannon: Lie down.

Paul: Give me a chance, woman.

He positions his arms by his side and tries to lie back, but he appears to be too wide.

Shannon: Cross your arms - everyone has their arms crossed.

Paul shoots her a dirty look before crossing his arms and easing his body down into the coffin. His feet hang over the edge.

Paul: (Triumphantly) See - this is not for me.

Bartender: Well... (thoughtfully) not necessarily.

Paul: It's uncomfortable... and tight.

Shannon: But you won't need your feet. It's not as if you'll be going anywhere.

Paul:(begins to wiggle) I don't fit.

The bartender bends down behind the bar and produces a saw.

Bartender: The feet can be cut.

Paul: (shouts) CUT?!

Bartender: What's the big deal. You're already dead.

Paul: I'm very much alive, thank you! (he wiggles) But I'm (pauses & wiggles) stuck. I'm stuck!

Bartender: Perfect fit, I'd say.

Paul continues to wiggle as Shannon takes the saw from the bartender. She stands at Paul's feet and looks down at them as though she is assessing the situation.

Paul: (shouting as he wiggles) I'm claustrophobic. (pause) Can't-brea-

Paul stops as he notices the saw in Shannon's hand. Shannon bends down and grabs his ankles. Paul howls.

ACT 3

Shannon holds Paul's ankles and he has begun to hyperventilate.

Shannon: For a grown man, you're very dramatic.

Paul: (breathing heavily) I need to get out.

Shannon: I was just adjusting your feet.

Paul's eyes widen. The bartender giggles.

Bartender: (holds up the JD bottle) A triple for your troubles (she adds more whiskey to Pauls unattended glass).

Shannon places the saw across Paul's mid-drift.

Paul: What the hell?

Shannon: I promise (reaching for her camera bag). I'll have you out in a sec.

Stage door slams open and all three turn to look. A dishevelled man falls through the door with a ripped white shirt and wearing a Hi-Vis waistcoat. He slams the door shut behind him and reaches up, bolting it. On the back of his waistcoat are the words COMPLIANCE OFFICER. He turns around and presses his back to the door, breathing heavily. There is loud jeering and banging at the door.

Shannon: What's going on?

Compliance Officer: Bloody animals.

The bartender rushes over to the door.

Paul: (shouts) Help me out mate.

Shannon: Protesting again?

Compliance Officer: Protestors don't bloody loot.

Shannon: (excitedly) They're looting?

Bartender:(shouts at the door) Fuck off - I've called the police.

Compliance Officer: I don't know why they make me wear this (he takes of the waistcoat). Makes me a flipping target.

The noise begins to move away from the door. Meanwhile, Shannon has begun to take photos of Paul from different angles.

Paul:(angrily) When I get out of here, I swear...

Bartender:(hisses at compliance officer) The police station is two minutes away... why come here?

The Compliance Officer begins straightening his torn shirt.

Shannon: (while taking pictures of Paul) I can see the headlines now...

Compliance Officer: We are trying to help. I mean, why wouldn't you want to stay home with your family? Give you lot an inch and you take a whole damn plane (exasperated). If you all would just follow the rules, this could be over quickly.

Paul: Mate, help me out.

Bartender: You lot?

The Compliance Officer reaches into his back pocket, takes out an envelope and hands it to the bartender.

Compliance Officer: I'm shutting you down.

Bartender: What? Why? (pause) You can't!

Compliance Officer: Yesterday, you were open at 10:15pm

Bartender: How did you...

Compliance Officer: Eyes everywhere (pause). Licence revoked with immediate effect.

Bartender turns to Shannon, who has walked over to the door.

Bartender: This is ridiculous. It was only me and her here.

Shannon: Will she have still access to the place?

Paul: (shouts) Can someone get me out of here?!

Compliance Officer: S'pose so.

Shannon: Great (to the bartender). I need to go get some shots of the freedom fighters. I'll collect that (she nods at the coffin) first thing tomorrow.

Shannon exits stage, while the bartender begins opening the envelope.

Compliance Officer: (shouts after Shannon) More like freedom blockers. They belong in an asylum!

Bartender: You can't shut me down. This is my livelihood!

Compliance Officer: Rules are rules love. (As he exits the stage, he shouts back) You can appeal.

The bartender rips up the letter and lets the pieces flutter to the floor.

Paul: Help me, please (desperately). I promise to wear a mask.

The bartender gives him a look of disgust before removing her apron and throwing it on the floor.

Paul: Wh-what are you doing?

Bartender:(opens the door) Joining the protest.

Bartender exits stage as the lights go down.

Paul:(Hysterical) No, please...

The End

Shara Cooper
The Witching Hour

'Take the next left.' The old woman nodded nearly imperceptibly at the turn that would take them off the wide boulevard and down a dimly lit side street.

The cabbie glanced at her in the mirror and then at the meter. What did he care, the old woman wondered. It's not like he was getting better fares at this hour.

The old taxi glided like a brick on oil across four empty lanes of traffic and waited at the turn signal. In the backseat, the old woman clutched her teal, leather purse on her lap, nails digging into the side. She gazed out the driver's side window, watching as the housing complexes grew rattier.

At one point this area had been new and full of anticipation for new beginnings. That was before even her time. She struggled to imagine what it had been like when it buzzed with fresh life. Buildings like these that were squeezed so tightly together probably appealed to young families, happy they could dabble in homeownership. Now they stood crumbling, unfit for the average person, but functional enough to house the unwanted, the mentally ill, the addicted.

'Park on the next block,' the old woman said. 'Right there, after the blue car.' She flicked a crooked finger at the space then folded her hand back on her lap. How quickly her body had betrayed her. At one time she had moved with confidence, free of the aches and the general wobbliness that plagued her now.

Her life had been carefree. Now she was decrepit, beaten down by a future filled with promise.

The cabbie compliantly manoeuvred the taxi into the parking spot and calculatedly locked the doors, an illusion of security from the outside.

'I thought we were going to Oakridge.' His eyes sought an explanation in the rear-view mirror.

'We will,' she said, frowning. 'I need to stop here for a minute.'
'I have to leave the meter running.'

She nodded curtly. She'd never thought otherwise.

A streetlight at the end of the block flickered intermittently.

Even without the flickering light the road was sparsely lit, long forgotten by the politicians that kept streets safe for voters. Few people that lived here ever found themselves in a polling booth.

The darkness gave the same muted effect as a soft blanket of snow, providing peace in its sheltering cover but also giving an eerie feeling in the absence of activity.

The witching hour. A wry smile passed briefly over the old woman's face. Every hour felt like the witching hour to her. The clock on the cabbie's dashboard read 3:07 a.m. Close enough.

Every inch of the block was consumed by brick. A heavy mass with doors and windows, marking a pattern along the monotonous surface. Front porches showed hints of the unique personalities they housed. Some were piled with recycling or refundable bottles. Others stored potted plants or bikes. On one stoop a mangy grey cat waited for a chance to slip inside.

She didn't need to count the fifth door from the left. That structure loomed at her as if it wanted to claim her. Inside the taxi's interior the cabin became suffocating and the old woman could feel her heart against her ribcage.

Above the townhouse's door was a wide window with a Juliet balcony. Twenty years ago that glass had shattered and everything in the old woman's world shifted. Air soured, gravity strengthened, and food dulled.

Back then, the unit had been filled with antiques. Not the kind that sold for thousands at auction houses, but the variety which housed bedbugs and fleas. Some had been cleaned up while others were concealed under piles of fabric and garbage.

The air had been thick with cigarette smoke, pot and incense as well as the choking smell of unwashed everything. When she'd entered the space, she'd wanted to open a window, but found it would only open a crack and was already ajar.

On the record player someone had been screeching Your head will collapse, But there's nothing in it, *And you'll ask yourself, Where is my mind, Where is my mind.* The old woman hadn't known the song then, but she knew every word now. Her daughter had slumped against the speaker stroking the surface, as though she wanted to meld with the music, absorbing it into herself, and then fading off into the distance as the notes dissipated.

The old woman, then a slightly younger woman, had clicked the system off and pulled her daughter's arm, forcing her to rise.

As she did, the threadbare housecoat had opened and showed a blanket of bruises. Purple, yellow, and blue mottled colour splashed across her body as if she'd been dragged across the wet canvas of a sunset painting. Stepping back the woman gaped, unable to look away. Her daughter hurriedly tied the robe, glaring at her mother.

'You can't keep living like this,' the old woman urged, her voice cracking with desperation as she tried to make her words register. 'You're going to kill yourself. Or he's going to kill you.' They stared at each other, exhausted, at an emotional impasse after years of constant deadlock.

The woman reached her hand out, offering it in peace, a benign

gesture. But on the inside, she desperately wanted to take her daughter and wrap her up, as she had once been, safe in her womb. If only she could go back in time. Whatever she had gotten wrong, she'd get right this time.
'Poppy, come home,' she pleaded. 'I'll take care of you.'
'Don't call me that!'

It was the wrong thing to say and the wall bricked up.
'Get out!' Her daughter grabbed the woman and shoved her violently toward the door. 'I don't want to see you again. I never want to see you! You don't understand me.'
The next day, when she bathed, the old woman would find her own metric of bruising.

'Ma'am. Are you alright?'

The cabbie looked at her anxiously. The old woman nervously smoothed her wool skirt and was surprised to find wet spots. She ran her fingers over them, wondering where they came from, until another drop fell, hitting her finger this time. She dried her face with the back of her hand and tightened her grip on her purse, pulling it into her abdomen.

'I'm fine.'

'Can we go? Are you waiting for someone?'

'I'm waiting. I need more time.'

She cast her eyes back on the building and then closed them.
***

Get your hands off me! The woman slapped her daughter across the face so hard that her head hit the wall. Cradling her cheek, she stared at her mother, eyes raging. She shoved her mother by both shoulders, pinning her against the wall. The corner of a table cut the old woman's side as she failed to stay upright. A lamp sailed past her, smashing behind her and glass raining at her feet. She ducked and moved toward the door, narrowly avoiding an ashtray.

You are crazy. What is wrong with you? You ungrateful little bitch! Everything maternal about her slipped out of reach as she defended herself from years of frustration and anguish. *After everything I've done for you!*

She reeled at her daughter slapping her again, this time causing her lip to split. Blood started to leak toward her chin.

Her daughter stopped and wiped at it. She stared at the red streak on her finger and then at her mother. For the first time in years, she looked stone-cold sober when they locked eyes.

I. Hate. You. Every word perfectly and clearly enunciated.

Ditto. The old woman growled back, walking toward the door. As she crossed the threshold, she felt her daughter's foot kicking her backside and she crumbled on the floor. Her daughter threw her mother's teal purse at her, the contents spilling at her feet. Unravelled in front of her was a vinyl accordion of pictures.

Her daughter in infancy, in the bathtub, playing the piano, with poppies braided in her hair, atop a pony, at graduation, and finally, at her wedding.

The old woman swooped her belongings together into a pile and started shovelling everything into her bag. Fiercely she zipped it shut and then lunged at the closed door.

You ungrateful little bitch! You are such an embarrassment to me. How I ever raised a daughter like you, is beyond me! I hope you do die, then at least, I don't have to think about you anymore! She screamed and pounded on the door, kicking it for good measure. *If you knew half the things I've done for you! And you choose to stay here, living like this, with that man.* Bile rose in her throat at the thought of him.

She stopped, breathless because she'd almost said what would Andy think of you now? Every rational thought evaded her but some remnant of intuition stayed. Bringing her dead son-in-law into it was unrecoverable. She kicked the door once more and bent to pick up her purse.

Something reflective caught her eye. Wedged between the floorboard and the wall was her watch. She picked it up and instead of feeling fury at the broken glass she felt exhaustion.

The kind of exhaustion that is cavernous, depleting you until you don't know if you have the strength to climb out of the hole that has engulfed you. The watch would read 3:19 a.m. forever.

On the sidewalk, she tried to fix herself up as much as possible.

Standing on the stoop trembling, she started rationalizing her role in the events. The racket continued inside as her daughter destroyed her own belongings. When it quieted, she looked up at the window and their eyes met. A look of grief, penned down by rage, passed between them.

The familiar sight of a yellow cab rounded the corner and the old woman hurried toward it, waving. When she looked back her daughter was gone.

****

'There was a murder there, 'bout twenty years ago.' The cabbie had rotated in his seat so he could look directly at her. 'You remember? I sure do. I was living just a couple blocks that way.' He waved in a direction to their right without taking his eyes off her. The old woman shivered and looked back at the block of townhouses.

'Here, I'll turn up the heat.' He rotated a dial before continuing.

'They say she killed herself, you know. She was brimming with opiates. They were surprised she'd been steady enough to walk.

I drove past it, you know, the scene, not long after it happened. Her body was still there, under a blanket. Glass everywhere… Saw the boyfriend too, leaning against a wall talking to a cop like it was a normal Wednesday. Did you know her?'

Perplexed, the cabbie studied the old woman.

In her hands she held the coil of photos that never left her purse.

The top image was of a girl sitting on a pony, her back ramrod straight as she stared intently down the lens of the camera. At one time, the image had been glazed with that soft glow that memories often carried, but now it was flat and two dimensional.

Her daughter hadn't wanted to stop riding, even for a picture. She'd been furious but had held herself still, willing to pose, but not smile.

'Everyone knew the boyfriend had killed her.' The cabbie gave up waiting for an answer. 'He used to smack her around. She'd stand at the corner, hiding bruises while begging for money.

Hooking sometimes too. The police could never prove it, they said he wasn't even home. But I think he had a row with her that night and she ended up being tossed out the window. How else could she get out there by herself the tiny thing that she was? No way she just fell through the glass. After that he walked around here like king shit. All entitled, like he knew he could get away with, well, murder. He done it for sure. '

The old woman wondered if the cabbie was trying to get a reaction out of her. He wasn't telling her anything she didn't already know. Reaching into her purse again she pulled out the broken watch, which still read 3:19 and now matched the clock on the dashboard.

'We can go. I gave you the address earlier.'

'Yes ma'am,' said the cabbie, relieved.

Whatever had happened that night after she'd left didn't matter to the old woman. She'd killed her daughter as truly as if she'd thrown her out the window herself. She'd been the catalyst, leaving her daughter unable to sober up, unable to fend for herself, unable to deescalate whatever had happened next.

They coasted past the flickering streetlight and as they rounded the corner the old woman took one last look at the building and saw the shadowy figure of a woman standing in front of the window gazing back.

The zipper on her old purse had long broken and the leather cracked. From it, the old woman pulled out a water bottle and three bottles of long-expired Percocet, prescribed after a hip replacement years earlier. The cabbie cranked up the radio and rhythmically tapped the steering wheel, happy to be on the road again.

'I'm sorry Poppy,' she whispered, popping the lid off the first bottle.

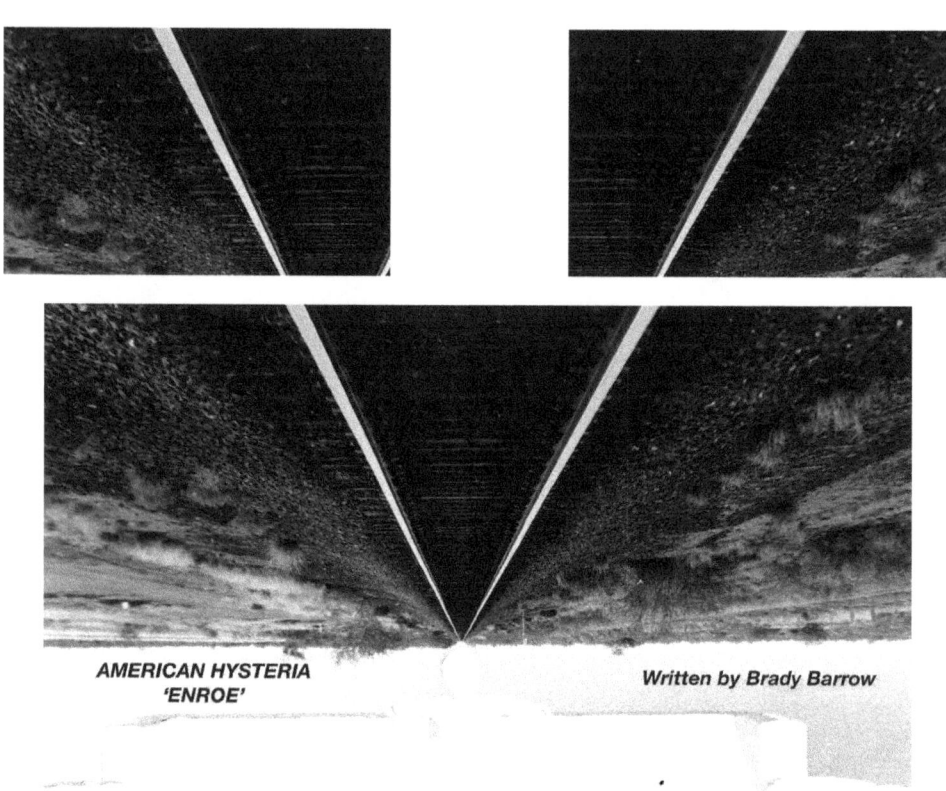

Brady Barrow
Enroe

Brady Barrow
Enroe

The West Texas town was small enough for everybody to know what kind of cigarettes each other bought and which sixteen-year-old-girl had a baby. With his six-string on back, Enroe walked to Big Bubba's surplus store in town every morning for a Coke.

'You got any good on that guitar, boy?' Big Bubba rolled a thick cigar-width cigarette.

'Real good.' Enroe flashed a gold canine.

'They should ship you over to Dallas. See what the city folk think of you.' Big Bubba pulled out a mason jar of sweet tea and another mason jar full of ice. He poured the sweet tea over the ice and it crackled and lightened the tea's complex. He took a big gulp, but nothing as impressive as Enroe's skills.

'Momma says the closest I'll ever get to Dallas is Terrell.' Enroe's face sunk.

'How's your Momma and Daddy?' Big Bubba asked, and Enroe just shrugged his shoulders.

'Now, I'm askin' you a question, boy.' Big Bubba leaned over the counter.

A woman in her early twenties stood patiently in line. She twitched a smile at Enroe. Big Bubba took out a handkerchief and wiped his red face. Enroe stared at the woman. He looked her head to toe real rude and in his head thought the only woman as beautiful as her was his mother. He felt a deep connection with this stranger, and she felt uncomfortable.

'Excuse me?' she said, firm yet polite. Enroe got out of her way and smiled with his gold chomps.

'Hi, Bubba.' She put a bottle of whiskey on the counter.
'Hello darlin', that all?' Bubba perked his chest and gave her a hospitable grin.

'No sir, some Marlboros.'

'Yes ma'am.' Big Bubba grabbed them quickly.

 She lit her cigarette before paying. She opened her bag, ashes dropped inside as she rummaged for cash.

'How's it goin'?' Enroe managed to squeak out to the woman.
'Goin' good, how you doin'?' She looked him straight in the eyes and Enroe lost his words. She waited for a second.

'Don't worry about him, he's a little slow. He ain't dangerous.'

Big Bubba smiled at the woman, but she turned her attention to Enroe.

'What's your name?' she asked.

'Enroe, E-N-R-O-E.'

'That's a real nice name. You dangerous, Enroe?' she said.

'A little.' Enroe stood up straight. 'What's your name?'

'Leyla,' she sang.

'That's a lovely name, nice to meet you,' Enroe spat out.

'It's nice to meet you too, Enroe. Would you like a cigarette?'

Enroe and the woman stepped outside, a distance from the gas pumps, and she lit Enroe's cigarette. Big Bubba kept a watchful eye from inside while he served the other customers
'How come I've never seen you before?' Enroe asked.

'I haven't been here real long or anything like that.' She smoked her cigarette and stared down the solo road.

'You oughta stay away from Hollywood,' Enroe warned.

'Why can't I go to Hollywood?' She stood with her brown curly hair past her shoulder blades and long denim skirt.

'Soon as they see you, they're gonna snatch you up, make you a real famous movie star.' Enroe exhaled his smoke.

'That's nice of you to say. You any good on that guitar, Enroe?'
'Real good.' Enroe took the guitar out from the gunny sack, then threw it down on the dusty earth. He thought for a moment, what

song would I play for an angel?

In the distance, a loud motor came rolling down the dirt road.

A real nice vehicle roared closer and closer. Leyla turned her attention to the car approaching the gas pump. A dapper man in a nice suit, big cowboy hat and boots climbed out the car.

'If you'd excuse me, Enroe.' Leyla put out her cigarette.

'Do you know him?' Enroe watched the urban cowboy bop his way over.

'He's my husband,' she said with a smile.

'You ain't got no ring on.' Enroe forgot what song he was going to play.

'I'll see you around, Enroe.' She turned to the cowboy and embraced him.

'You good on that guitar, boy?' The cowboy gave him a white Texas smile.

'He's real good, ain't ya Enroe?' Leyla had her arm looped in the cowboy's arm, which gave Enroe extra heat in his bones.

Enroe stared at the couple and the music of the angel was out of Enroe's soul. Instead, the music of the devil was close to the surface of Enroe's being. He clenched his muscles and refused to play for Leyla and her cowboy.

'Maybe next time.' The cowboy tipped his black hat at Enroe.

'Why you ain't bought Leyla a ring?' Enroe clenched his jaw.

'What you say, boy?' He looked at Leyla and she narrowed her eyebrows at the cowboy. He took a couple steps towards Enroe.

'Men like you don't deserve a woman like Leyla!' Enroe yelled loud enough for Big Bubba to hear from inside the shop. He took one step towards the cowboy to attack.

The cowboy turned around quick and jacked Enroe right in the eye with a stiff, sharp hook. Enroe fell for what he thought was forever. He hit the dirt hard and the cowboy stood above him. Leyla slowly walked back to the cowboy's car.

The surplus store watched passively. Big Bubba didn't even have his hand on his rifle. The cowboy leaned down and got in Enroe's face. He nodded his head a couple times, taking in Enroe's features. He grabbed the boy's short hair and pulled his head in close.

'I never wanna see you again, you hear me?' The cowboy spit when he said 'see'. Enroe stared at Leyla in the cowboy's car.

'What's your name?' he asked.

'Enroe,' he said, shaking.
'Can you spell it?' The cowboy felt pity.

'No sir.' Enroe couldn't remember.

The cowboy whispered, 'I shot a man in Waco, just to watch him die. Don't fuck with me, now.' He let go of Enroe's hair, and the boy flopped down on the dirt. The cowboy threw a quarter on Enroe's stomach and walked to the gas pump.

Enroe walked far to the tree next to the railroad track. He sat, watching trains go by, and couldn't think of a single chord or note to play. He listened to the rocks shift under the steel wheels on the railroad. The locus chirped and the sunset started to drop down the hills in the West.

His eye ached. He permanently winked at the landscape. He wanted to sleep under the tree. But he heard the music of his father, and it was urgent. With one eye, he looked deep into the southern, amber sky. He saw her eyes everywhere on the walk home.

Enroe walked from the farm to the surplus store the next morning to get his Momma some things. He left his guitar at home. Momma told him, grab the things quick, and didn't give him any extra money for a Coke. But Enroe had the quarter from the cowboy.

He got to the store around lunchtime and marched his swollen face into the store. There was a nice, funky twitch in the air that made Enroe feel lightweight. The weather had cooled off from the day before and the shop's faces were welcoming. Even Big Bubba had a big smile when he saw Enroe.

'You alright, Enroe?' Bubba asked.

'I'm good.' Enroe grabbed a Coke from the cooler and slapped the cowboy's quarter in front of Bubba.

The loud roar of the motor filled Enroe's ears. It was a ringing mixed with the deep rumble of a buffalo. It filled Enroe to the brim with heat. The cowboy, in a sky-blue suit and white boots, held the door open for Leyla in her fancy, sharp heels. She had on a white blouse with a yellow skirt. There was a mantra in Enroe's brain, a rhythmic and tense sound that felt good.

The couple walked towards the store and the cowboy walked into the shop before Leyla, which raised the heat in Enroe. The cowboy had a Dallas smirk and his gold buckle reflected in the midday sun. His face was red, and his breath stank of vanilla sarsaparilla and whiskey.

'Is that you, boy? Almost couldn't recognise you.' He laughed and patted Enroe on the shoulder, booze trailing from his breath. Enroe gripped his Coca-Cola tight, staring at the cowboy's temple. Leyla grabbed two Cokes from the fridge and cracked both bottles.

'Donny, let's have a Coke.' Leyla handed the cowboy the drink. Enroe cracked open his bottle and took a nice sweet gulp of syrupy gold. The store was silent and the three drank their sodas while Bubba held his right hand on his rifle from behind the counter.
'Listen, buddy. Real sorry about yesterday. No hard feelings?'

Donny held out his hand and Enroe gripped it. 'Got yourself some good-lookin' teeth, son.' Enroe held his smile.

Leyla jumped in.

'Bubba, would you help Donny out with his car? It ain't workin' right.' She smiled at Bubba.

'Let's go take a look.' Bubba grabbed a Coke and went to the car with Donny.

'Hello, Enroe,' Leyla said. 'Help me,' she whispered.

'I don't know nothin' about cars.'

'You need to help me get rid of him.' She looked out at Donny beside his car. Enroe drank the rest of his Coke quickly.

'I need to grab some things for Momma and go home.' Enroe plonked the Coke bottle down on the counter.

'Enroe, please, I can't do it without you. You don't know what he does to people.' She gave him sad eyes.

'Leyla, my Momma will—' Enroe started but Leyla got real close, closer than any woman besides Momma had been to Enroe.

'We'll take his car, his cash, and head straight for the border. You and me. But I don't know this town. Can you take us somewhere secluded?' She stared deep into Enroe's swollen eye. He thought about the beach in Mexico, him and Leyla. Not once in his twenty-something years did Enroe consider leaving Texas.

'There's a tree by the railroad track west of here,' Enroe whispered.

'How far?'

'Maybe thirty minutes, just down the road.'

'Take us there, please, Enroe.' She waited for him to respond for a couple seconds.

'Stay here.' Enroe walked outside towards the car.

'That should do it, Mr Walker.' Big Bubba wiped grease on his trousers. Donny Walker pulled out a hundred dollars and gave it to Big Bubba.

'Apreciatecha Bubba.' Donny took a sip of Coke and Bubba walked inside full of life.

'That's a real nice car, Donny. Never seen a car like that. My Daddy had a Ford T Model but we sold that.' Enroe soaked in the car's potential.

'She's a mighty fine stead.' They both laughed.

'You need a driver? Can't imagine anything nicer than drinkin' whiskey in the back of one of these cars with a nice lady, shoot.' Enroe wiped a finger on the hood.

'You any good at driving, boy?'

'Real good.'

Donny gave Enroe a two-dollar bill. Inside of the shop, Leyla restocked on Marlboros and leaned in towards Big Bubba.

'Bubba, I need you to help me.' She lit a cigarette while Enroe played Donny outside.

'How you much you pay for this chariot?' Enroe walked around the beast.

'Not a goddamn dime.' The cowboy reached down and dusted off his boots. He reached into the backseat and grabbed a bottled beer. 'Beer?' He held a cool one out.

'No, sir. Gets dangerous on these roads.' Enroe kept making small talk until Leyla came outside the store gingerly.

'You boys kiss and make up?' she yelled from a couple feet away.

'Somethin' like that.' Donny smiled at Enroe. 'We got ourselves a chauffeur, darling.'

'Donny Walker letting somebody else drive his precious jewel?'

Leyla tucked her chin in and raised her eyebrows.

'What do you say? How 'bout a country drive?' Enroe held the backseat door open and bowed. Donny drunkenly crawled in and kicked his boots up on the cream seats.

'If you say so. You alright with that, Enroe?' Leyla leaned into the driver's side window. Enroe nodded and gripped the steering wheel. He wrapped his calloused fingers around the leather circle, hard. Daddy never let Enroe drive the Ford truck.

'Enroe, you lived here your whole life?' Leyla sat leisurely in the backseat.

'Yes ma'am.' Enroe cruised down the road.

'You ever gonna leave?'

'I'll go to the Stockyards in Fort Worth to sell some cattle when I inherit my Daddy's farm. Then I'm gonna die here.'

'I like you, Enroe. You don't shit from your mouth.' Donny passed the bottle and Enroe took a big swig. He hadn't ever had champagne before, let alone good champagne. The bubbles melted the dryness in his throat. It was like a tart Coke, he thought. But he knew it was expensive and that added to its gold flavour.

He drove far away from the town, towards the spot under the tree. He thought about how his knees ached from walking the distance home. Enroe played the scene in his head over and over. He would shake his head so he could see the road, the image of Donny Walker's hot blood was that strong. Leyla's words were printed on Enroe's retinas, promises even he, despite what little he knew, couldn't shake as sounding too good to be true.

But Enroe was already heading towards the tree and his music was written. It was clear and decisive and made him think about making love to Leyla. He thought about her long hair on her naked shoulders and then the images shifted to Donny Walker's brains marinating on the hot leather seats.

'You won't find these views in Dallas, shoot doggy.' Donny took off his cowboy hat and the wind blew his hair back. Donny sat up urgently. 'Look at those whitetails.' He pointed out the window so Enroe and Leyla could see the deer eating grass from about thirty yards away. Donny reached under the seat and pulled out a Colt revolver. As somebody once said: God made man, but Sam Colt made man equal.

He closed one eye, took a deep breath, and aimed at the Texas white-tailed deer. 'Enroe, you keep drivin' boy, don't you slow down!'

Leyla's path was obstructed, and she had panic coursing through her system.

'What the hell are you doing?' She tried to grab his shirt but Donny stuck his torso out the car window. Enroe checked the rear-view mirror and stared at the big wad of cash hanging out of Donny's back pocket.
'Don't slow down, boy!' Donny Walker fired off his revolver and blew the deer's face off. It reminded Donny of his invincibility and the bodies chucked in the Rio Grande. He hollered and

marvelled at his shot. 'Better shot drunk, I'll tell you, boy.' He grabbed Enroe's shoulder. 'You see that shot, boy? Stick around and I'll teach ya' couple things.'

Enroe's shoulder was burning, but he ignored the sensation and presented his gold teeth in the rear-view mirror.

Farah Nehmé
The Mogul Attacks

Benjamin Tickner
A Misremembered Moon

Hands clamping over her damaged optical receptor, Fizz retreated into the shadows of the dim alleyway. The human lurched towards her, swinging his improvised weapon from side to side as a warning, eyes wild. Supporting herself as she lowered herself warily, Fizz kept one hand pressed to her eye. Metal teeth bared, she retreated, deeper and deeper into the alley.

'Back away, you little robotic freak!' the human growled, face vehemently red. Pink and purple neon reflected off the puddle at his feet. He feinted forwards, before striking at her. Her systems protested at the sudden stress, frantically reporting damage to her torso and upper arm. 'Get lost!'

Fizz reeled backwards. She crashed onto the ground heavily, falling onto her side before scrambling upright once more. Thin vapour from the sewers shimmered towards the darkened, stormy sky. After a moment more to consider her options, she turned about and fled. Alleys and avenues branched out into each other and led to the same closed spaces, over and over again. At last, she came to an empty plaza that overlooked a steep, deadly drop into the accumulator fields at the base of the city. Even at a thousand metres up, Fizz could see errant electricity arcing between the pylons. Footsteps thundered after her. She twisted about, dropping low and hurrying behind a towering tree, the plaza centrepiece. The holographic leaves flickered, faint turquoise lights brightening the plaza with a sickly aura.

Fizz crouched closer to the ground, burying herself into the shadows at the base of the tree. Her extraneous lights faded as she went into low-power mode. Her hydraulics tensed up. The footsteps grew louder as the human came into the plaza, drawing up at the top of some steps. Two others flanked him. There was a sharp click, before the gentle whine of a hard-light pistol charging up echoed around the place.
She froze.

'Where are you, freak?' the one at the front called out, before gesturing sharply to his friends. They spread out, the first one heading straight towards the tree, the others following the edges of the plaza to cut off her escape. The humans prowled about menacingly. It would only be a matter of time before they found her. Face down in the entirely odourless synthetic soil that the tree was planted in, Fizz let her fingers slowly close around a handful of the stuff.

'Turn around. Let me watch those lights go out.'
The plastic muzzle of the pistol pressed into the back of her

head. A hand wove into the wires at the nape of her neck, tugging her onto her feet. Fizz spun about and threw the soil into his face. The hard-light pistol fired wide, and a hole cut through the trunk of the tree. The holograms at its top winked out one by one, plunging the plaza into darkness. Fizz barrelled past the human and once more into the labyrinth of side streets. She paused, only to twist around and bare her teeth again, unleashing a roar that was pure, artificial noise. Then she fled. Darkened pathways stretched out before her. After racing down an alleyway and encountering a dead end, she squeezed and squirmed through a small gap between two whirring ventilation units. The sounds of pursuit came after her, before rushing past. Fizz took a moment to calm herself, before moving on further forward.

Emerging on a translucent acrylic walkway, she reactivated her extraneous systems and, after some hesitation, the dormant AI core. At this moment, she needed all the help she could get. 'Oh, hello. Looks like all that bravado about not needing me last time has come back to bite you, hasn't it?' the AI started haughtily. Fizz doubled over and closed her working receptor, regret running through her system instantly. 'Well, well, well, look at the state of you. Had a little bit of a run-in with some disreputable types? So much for little Miss "I can look after myself, thank you very much".'

'Cricket... not... n-not right now,' she whispered, 'Please. I... I need you.'

'If you wanted me to run a diagnostic report, I've already done so, and I can tell you that it's not good. Aside the obvious damage to your left eye and right arm, there are other errors that you ought to repair at your earliest convenience.'

'I know, look, I-I want to go home. Can you just tell me the quickest route?'

'Already sorted, I'll put the directions into your solid-state drive. I suppose now you'll turn me off again, seeing as I've served my purpose for the moment? Another indiscernible amount of time offline, such joy.'

'N-No, I… I just want someone to talk to.'

She started to walk, following the directions Cricket had uploaded into her memory, before urging herself to ignore the pain and jog. A peal of distant thunder heralded the onset of rain, and with the early hours of the morning bringing a few fingertips of natural light down between the buildings, the city at last willed itself to sleep. It was a short, and thankfully uneventful journey.

'So, what did happen, if you don't mind me asking?'

Fizz ran a hand through her fibre optic hair, sighing. Out of the corner of her eye, she spied a mirrored sheet of glass, and turned towards her reflection. Sparks sputtered out of her damaged receptor. Wincing, she brushed her fringe down to conceal it. The other remained as it always was - deep, black, and emotionless. She turned her attention to the other damages.

One of the auxiliary hydraulic tubes in her arm had split, limiting the fine motor functions of her right hand. She lifted the ratty brown poncho - the only clothing she had found, two sizes too large, one servo shoulder poking out of the neckline - and gingerly inspected her torso. A rupture, where the weapon had struck, let some wires spill out, and some had broken apart. Frightened, Fizz went to touch them, but as soon as her fingers graced the inner workings, she drew back and averted her eye.

'A lot happened. I guess… I got careless.'

'You? Surely not. Why, you've always been the very model of delicate and restrained.'

Rebuttal faltering, she continued moving, descending a stairwell that went down onto an empty street. Neon in five shades of orange illuminated disused shopfronts. Her destination was only ten minutes away - she had been closer than she had thought. 'You stole something, didn't you?' Cricket asked, accusingly. 'You let your guard down because you needed something, and whoever you took it from didn't appreciate being pickpocketed by a robot.'

Fizz glumly reached under her poncho and pulled out a broken phone. She toyed with it slowly, letting the luminous reds catch across its surface. She sighed once more, letting it fall out of her hand and clatter on the floor. It hardly seemed worth the trouble. 'Well, it doesn't matter either way: we're here. The doors are still electronically locked, however there is a window open round the corner. I don't think anyone was expecting you at this time of day. Chances are, you'll be all alone.'

The Ninth District Laboratory was dark and dormant, its sleek, slate grey shape perched over the yawning drop down to the capacitor banks far beneath the city. The double doors were closed, a panel at its side flashing navy blue. Fizz lifted her hand, palm up, and examined it. Her fingers curled closed. She took Cricket's advice and entered via the window, directly into the room where she wanted to go. The interior was cold and clinical, but with a floor made with planks of replicated alpine wood. Fizz looked around mutely. The overhead lights snapped on and the door opened. Professor Hasse stepped into the room, cleaning his glasses with a cloth. He set them on the bridge of his nose and shortly pulled on his beard. Upon noticing Fizz, his eyes widened dramatically, his mouth opening into an 'O'.

'Good grief! What happened to you?' he approached her urgently, hands hovering over her shoulders. It almost seemed like he was afraid to touch her. She smiled softly.

'Hello, professor.'

'Yes, yes, there'll be time enough for all that once I get a proper look at you. Sit up here and I'll attend to you presently. My goodness, you have been in the wars. Did Cricket give you a diagnostic report?'

The AI was uncharacteristically silent, almost sullenly so. 'Yeah,' Fizz pulled her poncho off over her head as she spoke, before hefting herself onto the desk that Professor Hasse had pointed out. His tools were in the same place as always, right beside her. She moved her fringe out of the way as he directed her to, careful not to touch the sparking remains of her receptor.

The professor went to touch it, but then decided otherwise. 'Dear, dear, this does look quite serious. These things can't be helped, I suppose. You should perhaps record this so that if I am not available, you can attempt some repairs yourself - I mean, there's an idea. I'll tell you what to do. Let me take a look at your arm first.'

Dutifully, Fizz extended it towards him, twisting her hand about and flexing her fingers experimentally. The extent of their movement was into a loose claw, rather than a fully closed fist. Professor Hasse directed her to connect the broken piping together and tape the split shut. Then, after flushing her hydraulic system, she tried to flex her fingers again, and they worked perfectly. She grinned at the professor, and he gently mirrored her expression.

'There, now. Nothing so major. It is a bit of a temporary measure, but it should be a couple of years before you'll need to look at it again. When we have more time on our hands, I will schedule in a maintenance appointment. Let us examine the other damages.'

Hesitating, she lifted her arm and revealed the rupture in her torso. The exposed wires continued to sputter. He knelt and pulled at his beard again. He bit his lip and glanced up at her. Fizz looked away, ashamed.

'What capacity are you operating at?' he asked.
'Nominal,' she answered hurriedly. 'It's not serious.'
Professor Hasse tipped his head to one side, crossing one arm over his body. She sighed and sagged.

'It's been better,' she said, bowing her head. The professor pushed his glasses up the bridge of his nose with his thumb. Attempting to occupy herself, she flexed and unflexed the fingers of her other hand.

'Usually, we would just get replacements for parts like this, but you happen to be custom-built. A lot of your parts are unique and take more effort than usual to be made. I'm afraid that this cannot be restored to perfect working order. But the thing that saddens me the most is that it happened to you. This certainly wasn't self-inflicted, or an accident. I'll try my best, but…'

Professor Hasse pushed his hair out of his face and straightened up. Fizz watched him move across the laboratory room and stare out of the window from which she had entered.

She angled herself so that she could get a look at what had caught his attention, before edging down onto the ground and walking towards him. The night sky above the city was black and featureless. A gibbous moon, isolated in space, waning infinitesimally. Something at the back of her mind told her that it was wrong, but she did her best to ignore it.

'You are special, Fizz. Perhaps more than I know. You're meant for remarkable things.'

'Yeah, well,' she shrugged, 'Sometimes it doesn't work out exactly like you planned. Maybe you were wrong about me. Maybe I'm too delicate for a world like this.'

'Oh, don't say that,' the professor turned towards her, softly smiling once more. 'Look, let's just get you fixed up, and we shouldn't have to worry about this. Nothing a little more tape can't fix.'

'Yeah.'

She made her way back to the desk and lifted herself back onto it, and Professor Hasse helped her seal up the rupture in her torso and package the wires back into place, before turning his attention to her optical receptor.

'Are there any other issues beyond the physical?' he asked, looking into its depths as she held her hair out of the way. 'Electronical faults, malfunctions, that sort of thing?'

'I-I… I have a problem with my memory. Sometimes I have trouble recording things properly. There are these blank spots in what I remember.'

'Ah, yes, you did mention that to me last time you were here. We're still working on a way around that. Unfortunately, we didn't pick up on it in the prototyping. You still learn things, don't you?

And you remember things in the immediate moment. Perhaps it's something to do with the encoding. Well, as I told you, there are certain time periods that you can select as 'key memories' to prevent loss. I would suggest that perhaps this little interaction of ours is one you might nominate for that. Thus, when you sustain any damage like this again, you'll know what to do. You can just take out the bits you don't need and then splice the remainders together so you're not just sitting here for several minutes at a time.'

She smiled. The professor did too.

'It's a good thing that we have a lot of these optical receptors. We use them for other robotics projects as they are my own design. It should be as simple as taking the old one out and slotting in a new one. There are some in the other room. Allow me to go and fetch one, I'll be right back.'

He turned about and headed out of the room. The lights flicked off.

'You're living a lie, Fizz. That was forty years ago,' Cricket said at last, crossly. 'You know as well as I do that the professor isn't coming back.'

Ignoring him, she pulled her poncho on over her head and followed the memory of Professor Hasse out into the corridor, and along to the room he would have entered. Reluctantly, Cricket pointed out a spare receptor on a dusty shelf. She picked it up, examining it from every angle, before ejecting the old one. Tipping her head back, she slotted the new one into the socket and tested it by altering the focus. Satisfied, she exited the way she had entered, meandering down an alleyway and finding a place where she could hang her legs over the drop.

'I can pretend he's still here, at least for a little bit,' Fizz pouted. 'You can do more than this,' Cricket responded, consolingly, 'You can't let a few minutes burnt into your hard drive define who you are forever.'

Lighting struck somewhere far off. As dark clouds roiled overhead, rain began to fall.

The Wind-Lover - Molly Hills

I've always hated the wind. Some people love it. It's actually a theory of mine that people are either born wind-lovers or wind-haters and there is just no in-between. I think the wind was the very first thing I hated.

You'll hear stories of the wind-lovers. Sailors standing proudly, squinting into the horizon on the decks of a boat, wind snapping at the sails, the clinking of the halyards against the mast.
I picture an English woman who married a sailor. She has furious red hair and lives on a Cornish cliffside and helps him build boats. I picture her standing on the quay in the morning, clutching a coffee, staring out to the sea. Her dramatic red curls whipping around her face. I would be a wind-lover too if I was her.

You hear about the Santa Ana winds in our Californian stories. 'Those Pesky Santa Anas', we say. As if to cartoonishly shake a fist at them. They bring the relief to the heat, but then they also bring the fires. Santa Ana. Saint Ana.

When the wind woke me up that night it was 3:00 am on the dot and one bird was singing. Just one. In the middle of a raging windstorm. My window had thrown wide open and I was scared. I felt so sick with anxiety, I couldn't get back to sleep at all. I couldn't stop hearing that idiot bird in between the gusts of wind and falling trash cans, singing its head off as if it wasn't even happening. A wind-lover, I suspected.

Maeve is a wind-lover, I thought. And so, I tried to think about Maeve. I imagined her sharing the bed with me and waking me up to listen to the gale. 'Emily, Emily, listen, outside!' she'd say 'it's so ANGRY out there! Doesn't the wind make you feel so cosy?' But it didn't make me feel cosy one bit. It made me wrought with anxiety and she could sense it, so she would slam the window shut and cuddle me back to sleep, whispering that we were safe, we were safe, we were safe. The wind made her feel cosy because she knew what it was like to be exposed to it, sleeping rough outside in it. But I hadn't known that about her yet.

I rolled over and surrendered to my phone in the hope of a data hit, to give me the dopamine I needed to steady my nerves. One new notification. Thank God.

How Bed Bath and Beyond are responding to COVID-19.

Not the dopamine hit I needed. I texted Maeve.

Can't sleep :(*are you awake?*

I slammed the window shut and watched the circle next to my message for it to light up with her face. Be there, be there, be there. It stayed grey. I agreed with myself I would wait until half past. But it stayed grey. She's not there. Something I already knew. Because that circle would never light up again.

Because Maeve would never be there again. Because she was gone. Taken in the night by an unexpected, unprecedented cardiac arrest at the age of 26, 2 years ago. No one knew the cause.

Unprecedented.

That's the word they use to describe this time. It's the word they use to describe everything we don't expect. Do we expect anything anyway? Isn't all of life, simply, unprecedented?

I wish I could text her about it. I would say *Maeve, don't you think this all sounds like a bad sci-fi movie?*

And Maeve would laugh and say I was so right. And she would probably say it was all a hoax anyway. Maeve liked conspiracies. I used to hate them. I would shout at her and we would fight about it. How she believed all printers were made to break a month past warranty. And that there were such batteries that could last forever but battery companies bought out the rights to them. Now I just miss her dumb theories. I miss our fights about them. And I miss her.

Because that's love really, isn't it? The real love. It's not the thing you're expecting. It's unprecedented.

Maeve used to always say that line from Sleepless in Seattle. You know that part when Meg Ryan's friend grabs her and goes *You don't want to be in love, you want to be in love in a movie.* Maeve shouted it at me every time I got hung up on a boy. And now I think, yeah. That's exactly it, Maeve. That's exactly it. Without even knowing it - the love I needed was shaking my shoulders shouting lines from romcoms right at my face. It was sharing dumb conspiracy theories with me. Platonic love. It wasn't romantic. It wasn't obvious. It was unprecedented.

And now here I am. With all of that love and nowhere to put it. The wind blasting at my closed window and the grey circle on my phone that will never again light up. I stare at it for a minute more. Damn those pesky Santa Anas. I throw open the window and let the wind yank at my hair. Leaning into it this time. That stupid bird is still singing. We are wind-lovers I say to it. And I'm pretty sure she says it back.

Carrying the Weight of Water
　　By Rebecca White

When's it going to rain, she begs. As if I could do anything about that. I stood in the gap where the patio doors lead out from the kitchen to the garden, cup of tea in hand. The steam from the tea matches the heat vibrating outside. She, the youngest one, sits on the floor at my feet watching for any trace to suggest the weather would break. Her long wavy hair flowing like crochet down her back, so stroke-able. But I don't touch it. I don't touch her.

The air is thick and muggy. Heat simmers over the paving stones. I've thrown open every window in the house. It's been like this for a month now. If only there was a breeze to move the stillness. August. We've made it to August, but could we get through it.

You can feel the weight of water in the air, she said. They said it would rain this afternoon, she said, I've been anticipating it all day. She watches the outside for any change. I change position and move away.

We're not just waiting for rain. We wait for test results, end of school results, university placement results, the end of lockdown and a safer world to move around in. And for whether we will be going to a trial next year.

We sleep with fans on high. They rotate in a semi-circle to push the air around each bedroom, buzzing like persistent mosquitos. We don't sleep well, whether it's from heat or dreams.

The younger one, at full stretch still a few inches shorter than me, had withdrawn into a cocoon. She'd go to her room, I guess she felt safe and in control there. I tried not to disturb her too much. She didn't talk, was just morose and hid behind her hair. I caught her crying a couple of times. I didn't realise it was a regular thing for her.

As soon as she told me what happened to her, she changed. She felt able to be around us again, or rather, to be herself around us. She relaxed, smiled even. I guess she was too young to realise what path her story was taking us on.

I wake early and go for a run before the heat of the day builds to a crescendo once more. It's busier than usual. 6:00am and people are everywhere. We were told to stay home which, of course, means we all go out. Most people stick to the main paths, but this is my turf, I know these woods like I know my expanding waistline, so I head off on the tracks amongst the trees.

I try to relax, breathe long and deep, arms down with gentle movement back and forth, legs stretched out and every stride lengthened and loose. Each foot rolled down through heel, ball, toe. It's not long before my breath gets quicker, shorter. Every stride a jumble as I jump over roots and fallen branches. Arms flail out to the sides for balance, shoulders up by my ears. I slip on tree roots barely noticeable above the grass. Up on tiptoes as there's not enough space to support a flat foot. My feet hurt; arches crushing, calves burning. The eldest one, I don't know how to get through to her. The younger one's easier, she's so much more visibly expressive, but this growing distance between me and the eldest is too much. She barely looks at me, or speaks. Why all this passive aggressiveness towards me? How can I support her through this? Rationalising all the hurt and pain she's holding inside I lose focus, I can't see where I'm going. I get too close to the branches and hold my arms up to shield my face. My eyes blur, brim over and splash down my cheeks while I run blindly through the woods. I push on upwards, uphill to pound it out of my feet, on my toes. Breathe. Don't forget to breathe. I breathe it out. Puff it out. Push it out. It's pointless.
Surrender, come on!
I give it up. I've reached the top. I'm out of breath. Chest heaving. There's nothing else I can do.

Give me the words to say. Give me opportunity to talk to her.

Give us something. Please.

I get home, take the key out of the zippered pocket in my leggings and open the front door. The eldest one is passing through the hall, cup of tea in hand. Head held in defiance, an inch or two above me now. I am irrelevant. The void between us palpable. I can't take it anymore.

If I've done anything to cause you hurt or anger, I am so sorry. Please tell me what it is so that I can understand.

Nothing, she said. I thought you were angry with me, she said, so I was avoiding you.

That's not possible. Not possible.

The youngest one is at the table bent over books. What are you studying, I ask. Boudicca, she said. She was a first century queen who, after the death of her husband, the king, raised an army against the Romans and tried to force them out of Britain because they had humiliated her and her people. She looks up from the book. What do they mean by, 'they humiliated her', she asked.

We give our statements. The anticipation was unbearable, we didn't know what to expect. Should I dress up and look professional to give the right impression? Or should I dress down to look relaxed, like it's no big deal. Of course it's a big deal! I've never done anything like this before. Never given a statement against someone I thought was a friend. It's obscene and unheard of and not something you ever expect to do. I couldn't stop shaking for four hours.

The detectives seem so young, professional yet trying to be informal, but it's still an unpleasant, complex and arduous process. We rake over all the details at least three times. I could hear the girls laughing with their detectives who were obviously trying to make the situation as light-hearted as possible. My detective and I barely laugh. Not that it was all serious, it just wasn't easy.

I had to say what emotional and psychological effect this was having on me. I know I repeated myself. I wasn't sleeping well and having nightmares. We all are. Of course I'm on edge, shaky. I find it hard to rest and switch off. Knowing He's out there. Knowing He will be making His excuses, changing His story, anything to make Him look good. I welcomed a man into my house and He treated my kids this way.

How can I rest until this is over?

The eldest one relaxes a bit after giving her statement, but it doesn't last long. She reins herself back in again and is pent up for weeks. She has exams, online exams. Not something we had anticipated. None of this was anticipated. It was a disaster.

We move around the house without interacting. Are we avoiding one another?

The youngest one's ability to give and receive physical touch starts to change. At first, she would come up to me and place one finger on my arm. It was her way of saying, I want touch but not too much. I suppressed my natural instincts and lightly placed my finger on her arm too. Another time she put her head on my shoulder and I stretched and bent my neck to place mine on top of hers. After a few weeks of messing about like this; fist pumping but not touching with open hands, or placing her arms around me at a distance to simulate a hug but without getting too close, she suddenly changed. She must have grown so comfortable with the simulation that she started to sit on my knee. I didn't stop her, even though it squashed my legs. She demanded attention and would not be satisfied until she'd wriggled her head under my arms so that I hugged her. I was afraid of touching her at first. She was really too big for this now, but maybe it was her way of turning the clock back and being younger again. Start from the beginning again. Then came the kisses to my cheek. She was back. Now I could give her a bear hug.

The eldest one, on the other hand, did not loosen her grip on her emotions until she was good and ready.

When I think of the things He did: His hands on her hips, His fingers stroking her thigh, how scared she was. How could He do these things to us? To them? How could He treat children this way? How could He…

My phone buzzes. My sister.

I'm having a hell of day, we had our PPE fitting. What a joke. Basically, we have an apron, glasses and a mask and there's not enough to be able to change between patients. How's your day?

Oh, you know. The usual.

Sitting here and not knowing what's going on with the investigation is scary, I tell the therapist. Putting all our pain into someone else's hands and trusting them to "fix it" is not a pleasant experience. All our personal and embarrassing experiences have been written down and could be read out in court. Now what? Are we free of it? No. Can we talk about it? No. We are doing well. Not bad, really. Focusing on the good things we can do, getting on with things.

Focus. I have to keep reminding myself.

I think of Boudicca a lot these days.

The close air yields some space. It's dark and purple beyond the kitchen. The girls notice the change, look up from their books and run outside. The air has finally broken and rain is chucking down from above. I watch them from the safety of the overhang at the back of the house. They sway in the downpour, relishing the liberation it brings, then frolic barefoot around the wildflowers in the ensuing mud. Still kids at heart, they give in to freedom and enjoy themselves, raindrops bursting onto their upturned faces like petals of a flower. Mouths open. I stay under the confines of the overhang.

The youngest one is changing and becoming more herself than she has been for over a year. It's freeing. For me. Hope is like rain, there's anticipation when the air is heavy with it, then relief when it is finally released. She told me a joke the other day. She held out her tee shirt. Feel this, she said. I brushed the soft cloth between my finger and thumb.

This is boyfriend material, she said and laughed. I looked at her. Incredulous. For an instant. Then burst out laughing.

A boy did that to me at school, she said. That's sweet, I say in return. She'd kept that one to herself, we've been in lockdown for months. She's affectionate again, loving, active and focused. She runs to the shops and then bakes. I'm in pursuit of the perfect brownie, she said.

An email arrives from the detective. The investigation is over and it has gone to the CPS. We now wait some more, anticipate more…

I watch my kids playing games with each other on their phones. Their bodies scattered on the sofa with legs intertwined. I wish I had the resilience of a child. The joy they find in life, in the small moments. We should bottle it up and dispense it to those fighting depression.

Most of the time I feel like I forget about it, I tell the therapist. I sometimes wonder if we are making a bigger deal out of it then we need to.

Laura Broadberry
Reflection

When Eleanor closes her eyes, she can almost see it again. The glamorous parties she used to throw, the elegant dresses she wore and the extravagance in every room. The vibrant atmosphere entertained a sleuth of guests on a regular basis. Almost daily.

All gone, snuffed out and abandoned.

Her precious home is now derelict, abandoned, in shambles. Sitting in the shadows of the early afternoon light, the sun is shining through where the windows had once been.

There had been polished cream tiles, marble columns and gold gilded coving beside the ceiling, now the tiles are dimmed and dusty, some of the columns are missing and the gold gilding is fading on the cracked ceiling. It used to be a welcoming entranceway, the electric atmosphere beaming with chattering guests before they entered the designated room. By comparison, the silence feels insufferable. Eleanor craves an obnoxious laugh to pierce the still air, wishing for someone to give her life a purpose again.

She doesn't remember how she got here, nor how she has the wine bottle in her right hand, which is almost empty. Her elegant scarlet dress from the night before gives the impression she hasn't changed since she lived here, but her bloodshot eyes and

smeared red lipstick would suggest otherwise.
Her hand trails along the bannister as she walks up the sweeping staircase, where the carpet is fading and destroyed by moths. The walls are bare, the portraits that loomed so large gone. Sold. What use does she have for her ancestors' portraits? Their expressions reminding her of the failure she's become.

Her feet carry her upstairs to the master bedroom. Oh, how she adored that room. Her private room to doll herself up in, taking pleasure in choosing which dress to wear and co-ordinating her makeup to match. She would admire herself In the mirror, flattening down any creases. The perfume she sprayed on to drive him crazy.
George Lambert.

From the moment they first met, Eleanor knew George was special. Someone to acquire and have on her side. Someone rich and powerful, despite being both herself. Someone that was hers. Her equal, her match. All eyes were on them when they entered a room, almost like they were royalty. Fawning over them, smiling at them, gushing about them. The attention intoxicating.

But perhaps she should've noticed his wandering eyes. Perhaps she should've seen how his hands lingered across other women's bodies. Perhaps she should've known his lust and free spirit couldn't be contained.

Or maybe she didn't care. Perhaps she saw how he paid other women attention and felt relieved someone else could deal with

him. Maybe she wanted to live in their fantasy world, where she could play the part of a rich, married woman. The perfect domestic housewife. The lady of leisure. Destined to be whisked away on a whim without a second glance.
She catches herself in the mirror, transfixed by the woman she sees reflected back.

A young woman had stood here once. Her blonde hair cascaded down her back in waves, telling people it was natural. In actuality, she spent hours using a range of products and appliances to achieve the look. She always considered her dark brown eyes boring, but eyeliner and eye shadow helped. Red lipstick to complete the look. Dresses gripped her slender figure, tailored to a precise fit. Heels of varying heights slipped on to complete the look. Even in her casual attire, she would wear heels, shorter heels preferably.

Here stands a different woman. Wrinkles beginning to form across her forehead. Her blonde hair a dishevelled mess. Her smeared lips tug downwards as the misery has taken over. Her dark brown eyes are lifeless and her posture drooping forward like a dying plant. She runs her hand down her dress, but her figure is no longer slender. The podge of her stomach is growing, whether that's from the alcohol or her growing age, she can't be sure. Her left hand settles on her stomach as she thinks once more about the lost opportunity.

If she asks herself the age-old question, she can't lie to herself. She used to put on a smile, give a hearty laugh, telling them that of course she loved George. But had she? Or had she fallen in love with an illusion?

A man who swore he'd be with her until death do them part, but neither are dead. Although, if she can see him for a moment, she isn't so sure he will be...

The brisk air slips into the room. She shivers despite herself and takes another long gulp of wine, hoping to drink away the memories. But as her eyes fall back on the mirror, she sees him, feels him. His lips caressing her neck, her collarbone, searching for her lips. His hands resting on her stomach if he wanted her company, or resting on her breasts if he felt horny. Depending on her mood, Eleanor would turn to face him and let him have his way with her.

'George, you bastard,' she says into the mirror, as if he can hear her. As if he'll run into the room and tell her to mind her language.

But he won't. He left.

The tears fall onto her dress, but considering the state she's in, tear stains are the least of her worries. She considers throwing the wine bottle at the mirror, but she grew up with the belief you should never waste alcohol.

A few moments pass, her fingers stroking the delicate outer rim of the mirror. Brushing with a gentle touch, like George once had with her. Tender, intimate, teasing her body until she could bear it no more; he would take the time to explore her, wanting her to experience pleasure. Even when he was rough with her, pulling, yanking, biting, leaving marks, he wanted her to enjoy it. Paradise.

A word they'd both thrown around as they laid together, back in those blissful early days. Hands searching, lips craving, bodies moving. The paradise would accompany them back then, watching as they held hands and smiled at one another. The world was brighter, easier, like floating along with the ease of a young child.

When had it changed?

After the honeymoon, when reality settled in? After their first anniversary, when he stumbled home with a half-hearted attempt at romance, promising to be better? After their newest neighbours moved in, when they just popped round to introduce themselves? Had he started having affairs then? Or had it always happened without her knowledge?

George still had a charm to him, smiling and laughing with their guests, holding her close and continuing to show her off. But once alone, the façade would fall away. He left her whenever possible. Avoiding her advances, sleeping as far away from her as possible, staying out late and returning with alcohol tainted breath.

She suspected something, but she hadn't wanted to acknowledge it. She wanted to be married, host extravagant parties and be included in the socialite world. She wanted them to be a dynamic duo, a power couple, a team, who functioned in a world of their own making. She wanted him to love, support and nurture her, like he promised on their wedding day. She wanted him to pick her up when she faltered and reassure her it'd be okay.

She wanted what she now knew never existed. A lie he told her, told everyone else. Had anyone else known? Or were they all as gullible as her?

She shakes her bottle of wine, hoping there's still some alcohol left, but nothing falls out. Walking over to the empty window, she lobs the bottle out and watches as it shatters upon the garden. Or at least, what had once been their garden. Now it's an unkempt mess, with overgrown grass, sturdy trees and dead flowers. She looks down, remembering the early days where she spent hours planting and watering her precious flowers, then choosing the best to give to George. He'd always appreciate it and kiss her in response.

She ends up back downstairs, going between rooms without much care. The kitchen no longer alive with chefs shouting at their staff. The library no longer occupied with people discussing important issues at length. The ballroom no longer filled with dancing couples and laughter. The conservatory no longer used to stare up at the night sky.

But she couldn't deny herself one room. The piano room. A cosy room she had loved, even as a child. With a fireplace crackling on the right wall from when you enter, the piano in the left corner furthest from the door. Two velvet couches adjacent to the door, in between a square oak table. There wasn't much else to the room, but nothing else is needed as all eyes would fall onto the pianist.

Eleanor always relishes in that. Even now, as she walks over and opens the cover. Her fingers trailing over the keys as she longs for the praise and applause. Her fingers move by instinct, remembering how to play the pieces she'd committed to memory. Despite the silence disappearing for the first time since she'd stumbled inside, the discomfort lingers, waiting for her to finish and be alone again. She plays and plays, but she knows she can't perform forever. She must leave her beautiful piano and the built-in furniture and the unkempt garden. She knows she must. But reflecting isn't the same as remembering.

Eleanor's therapist will be proud of her for facing her emotions. Facing her past. Facing herself. Although, she'll frown for the breaking and entering. The mansion her and George had settled in but had always been hers. The mansion her family has owned for centuries now fallen into disarray. The mansion that will be owned by the National Trust for all to admire and praise as they explore.

But they won't understand the artifacts or the paintings or the furnishings. Not when she destroys them, legacy be damned. The Williams' name will die with her, the sole heir to the fortune.

She takes one last look at the doorway she entered first, seeing the ghost of her memories haunt her before she stumbles back outside.

This will be the final time she can swear and shout and do as she please to her home. The final time she can return before it's sold, but what is the use when she died the day he left?

Zoë Coleman
Untitled

Annabel Yates

I am currently undertaking my Creative Writing MA, after receiving a First-Class Undergraduate Degree in English Literature and Creative Writing at Kingston University. I won the 2019-2020 Creative Writing Prize.

Benjamin Tickner

Creative writing has been my main passion from an early age. Fantasy is my preferred genre, but I always enjoy exploring new styles. I hope to become a published author

Brady Barrow

I was born in Texas and grew up in California. My inspirations range from Raymond Carver and Ernest Hemmingway's short stories to movies by Quintin Tarantino and Kevin Smith. I'm also inspired by musicians J Cole, Led Zeppelin, Kendrick Lamar, Miles Davis and my big brother Brett.

Caylyn Sheldon

Originally from the United States, Caylyn Sheldon studies Museum and Gallery Studies at Kingston University. She is currently writing a collection of poetry and a historical fiction novel.

Emily Troy

Emily Troy is a Historic Building Conservation student who writes in her free time, originally from Liverpool she moved to London in order to study at Kingston.

Farah Nehmé

Farah Nehme, a Lebanese illustrator and ideator.
I wore many creative hats in the fields of advertising, animation and technology.
As part of reinventing my approach to art making, I enrolled this year in the Illustration MA program at Kingston University.
I'd love to work on a variety of projects ranging from surface design to window displays and everything between and beyond.

Fiona Paterson

Fiona is a Publishing student who recently got back into creative writing. These poems are a product of lockdown #1 and reflect her mood at different moments.

Grace Watts

I am a first year media and communications student and have always had a passion for photography. Creating media gives me the chance to view the world and society in different and more creative ways, helping to expand and enhance my love for taking photos and capturing moments.

Isabelle Gray

Isabelle Gray has always loved poetry, but it wasn't until starting her Publishing MA and getting involved with RiPPLE, that she decided to share her work.

Katie Harnden

Katie Harnden is a second year Design Marketing student who enjoys exploring creative writing, learning new languages and travelling in her free time.

Kulsy Kashmiri

I'm a sci-fi nerd, coffee addict and cat lover. I write to find beauty in the ugly and draw to illustrate the strange world as I see it.

Laura Broadberry

Laura Broadberry is a postgraduate publishing student at Kingston University. She spends her free time reading books, writing fantasy stories and collecting stationery. You can find her on Twitter (@LauraBroadberry) or Instagram (@laurabroadberryreads).

Matthew Delaney

A Carshalton-born writer and aspiring teacher often found searching for the meaning of life and decent Russian Caravan tea! Loves screenwriting, cats, autumn rain, retro-futurism and dodo birds. 'For Edith'.

Molly Hills

Molly is from London and studies English Literature at Kingston. She works part-time as a chef and also as a horse trainer. She runs a monthly literary newsletter called Left on Read and enjoys taking on more commitments than she actually has time for.

Morgan Bratli

When not studying film and literature, Morgan Bratli dwells in Norway where he spends his time practicing ancient Viking traditions. These are most commonly known as reading and writing; not invading England with axe and shield.

Rachel Essex

I am a second year Creative and Professional Writing student with a passion for storytelling. I have been documenting my life and creating new ones through short stories, books and poetry since I first picked up a pen.

Rebecca White

My inspirations include Kate Bush, Anne and Emily Bronte and, let's face it Shakespeare. Experimental theatre, the Jamie Lloyd Company; Max Porter's 'Grief Is The Thing With Feathers'; my kids; alternative music and, most of all, dancing!

Rianna Davidson

Hey my name is Rianna, I am studying media and communication. I love editing and creating images that speak out. An image can create conversation, opinions and discussions, I want to be able to create content and base it on other people's experiences and also my own.

Sara Bouda

Sara Bouda lives in London and is an MA student taking Creative Writing in 2020/21. Her passions are wide, varied and unexpected. She hopes you enjoy her Ripple poem.

Shara Cooper

Shara is a Kootenay-based writer who likes open-ended questions and complex moments. She likes telling stories that are open to interpretation and reflect real-life experiences. She lives with her two daughters.

Sim Dyer

After spending several years working in Accounts, Sim decided to pursue her passion for writing at Roehampton University, where she graduated with a first-class degree in English and Creative Writing. Currently, Sim is studying for an MA in Publishing & Creative Writing at Kingston University.

Skye Price

You'll find me cosied up with a book or a film, alongside my cat, after a day of teaching English and Drama. Writing is how I process myself and the world around me. My aim is to equip my students with the same tool.

Stanimir Dimitrov

Stanimir Dimitrov is a trilingual Bulgarian from Austria. He is enrolled at Kingston University London with Creative and Professional Writing. His passion is writing poetry and stories and reading books.

Zoë Coleman

My piece is a digitally composed collage of illustrations created to document street scenes and intricacies of everyday life around Tooting and south London.

www.ingramcontent.com/pod-product-compliance
Lightning Source LLC
Chambersburg PA
CBHW040311050426
42449CB00019B/3481